In proud, vibrant Catalonia, food is what brings people together—whether neighbors, family, or visitors. By the sea, over a glass of chilled vermouth and the din of happily shared homemade *pica-pica* (tapas), is where you'll find the most authentic Catalonia. The region in northern Spain is known for its wildly diverse indigenous ingredients, from seafood to *jamon Ibérico* to strains of rice, and its richly flavored cuisine has remained unique throughout Catalonia's complex and fraught history.

In *Catalan Food*, chef Daniel Olivella, a native, serves enriching historical narratives alongside dozens of evocative photographs and eighty carefully curated recipes that are simple, freshly sourced, and intended to be cooked leisurely and with love—the Catalan way. Featuring traditional dishes like *Paella de la Barceloneta* (Seafood Paella) and *Ànec a la Catalana* (Duck with Prunes and Pine Nuts), as well as inventive takes on classics such as *Tiradito amb Escalivada* (Spanish Sashimi with Roasted Vegetable Purées) and *Amanida de Tomàquet amb Formatge de Cabra* (Texas Peach and Tomato Salad with Goat Cheese), *Catalan Food* brings heritage into any home cook's kitchen, where this regional fare was born. To know a culture, you must taste its cuisine; none is more rich and stunningly delicious than Catalonia's.

CATALAN FOOD

CULTURE & FLAVORS
from the MEDITERRANEAN

CATALAN FOOD

DANIEL OLIVELLA

WITH CAROLINE WRIGHT

PHOTOGRAPHS BY JOHNNY AUTRY

CLARKSON POTTER/PUBLISHERS
NEW YORK

Library of Congress Cataloging-in-
Publication Data
Names: Olivella, Daniel, author. |
Wright, Caroline, author.
Title: Catalan Food : culture and flavors
from the Mediterranean / Daniel Olivella
and Caroline Wright.
Description: First edition. | New York
: Clarkson Potter/Publishers, 2018. |
Includes index.
Identifiers: LCCN 2017048094 |
ISBN 9780451495884 (hardcover) |
ISBN 9780451495891 (ebook)
Subjects: LCSH: Cooking, Spanish—
Catalonian style. | LCGFT: Cookbooks.
Classification: LCC TX723.5.S7 O37
2018 | DDC 641.59467—dc23

LC record available at
https://lccn.loc.gov/2017048094

ISBN 978-0-451-49588-4
Ebook ISBN 978-0-451-49589-1

Printed in China

Book and cover design by
Stephanie Huntwork
Cover photographs by Johnny Autry

10 9 8 7 6 5 4 3 2 1

First Edition

To Paco, who gave me the *mise en place* for my career
—D.O.

To Paul, the unsung hero of this book, and always.
All my love, XOX
—C.W.

CONTENTS

INTRODUCTION
THE FLAVORS OF MY SKIN

I can still hear the pestle on the mortar. That *clack* and *scrape* will forever be in my bones. As a kid in Spain, I could hear that sound from all the way down the street when I came home from school. Mama was in the kitchen making *picada*.

I grew up in Catalonia, in the northeast corner of Spain near Barcelona. Like other Catalan kids, I hung out with my mom in the kitchen quite a bit. I've always loved to eat, and my mom first taught me how to taste. I can still smell our fire-roasted peppers, onions, and eggplant to this day. We cooked these foods with our neighbors in the center of the village on the outskirts of Vilafranca del Penedès. Grapevines grow everywhere in Penedès, and they gave our fires—and our food—a distinctive, smoky aroma.

We didn't have as many financial resources in Vilafranca as they did in the region's capital, Barcelona. Instead, we were rich in natural resources. So much incredible food grows in Catalonia, and when I grew up there in the 1970s, most people worked in the food trade as grape farmers, olive farmers, bakers, fishermen, or *cansalader* (meat curers). Once a week, these food producers would come to town and my mother would bring home olive oil, wine, sausages, whole fish, and even live animals like rabbits and roosters. We would keep the animals for a few days and then enjoy them for weeks afterward. We appreciated every part of the animal. When springtime came and the weather turned warm,

my friends and I knew the vineyard grapes were starting to bloom by the sweet perfume of violets and melons in the air. We knew where the richest muscat grapes grew, and we would pluck them and eat them. With so much amazing food at my fingertips, Catalonia gave me the flavors of my skin.

All kids are born with different *inquietuds*, yearnings, and food is definitely one of mine. So is travel. I had a fire inside me to see different places, meet new people, and learn new languages. Also, I longed to escape the oppression of Spain's military dictator, Francisco Franco, who ruled the country with an iron fist when I was growing up. Spain borders on France and, fortunately, I got the opportunity to study there through a school exchange program. In France, my long-standing love affair with crisp, tender baguettes grew even deeper. My dad had a good friend in Germany, so I was able to travel there as well, furthering my lifelong weakness for pork sausages.

When school ended, I was a bored teenager who needed something to do. It seemed my only prospects in Vilafranca were to become a house painter or a bike messenger. Luckily, my cousins came to visit from America at exactly the right time, and my parents suggested I go back to Chicago with them. My uncle Paco had a restaurant there, La Paella. After a half second's thought, I decided to leave Catalonia for Chicago. I left to discover the world and to find freedom from the narrow-minded thinking Franco had imposed in Spain. I hadn't even considered a career in food, but at my uncle's place, I worked as both a waiter and a cook. And I studied saxophone at the American Conservatory of Music. My *big* dream was to make it in music.

Cooking came to me so easily and I worked at a bunch of Chicago restaurants at the same time to pay the rent. My music career wasn't taking off, and I was becoming more and more enchanted with the craft of cooking. I heard through the grapevine that San Francisco was the place to be. This was the mid-1980s, and the food scene was exploding there. Alice Waters, Jeremiah Tower, and other chefs were shifting their focus from fussy French dishes to simple food made with high-quality ingredients from local organic farms. The wine industry was booming, and northern California reminded me of Catalonia. Plus my saxophone teacher was living in San Francisco at the time. I thought I could pursue both food and music there, so I picked up and moved again.

By the time I got to northern California, I had internalized the chef's general philosophy of *mise en place*—basically, getting your shit together. But when I started working at Zuni Café in San Francisco I began to understand what it means to be a professional cook. The Café's phenomenal head chef, Judy Rodgers, generously shared her intuitive cooking wisdom with me, teaching me the simplicity of an onion, a cut lemon, and a beautiful piece of wood. We never put more than five or six ingredients on a plate, and if you could make a dish with just anchovies, olive oil, and cheese, you were a genius.

After seven years of cooking at Zuni Café, Thirstybear Brewing, Delfina, and a handful of other great restaurants, I took a big leap. In 1999, I became a chef-partner in B44, a Catalan bistro in the heart of San Francisco's financial district. At the time, no one was representing Catalan food properly in America. No one was capturing how festive it was, rooted in sharing a drink and a laugh with your neighbors over little bites of food or a pan of paella for everyone to dig into. I thought it was time for Americans to enjoy Catalan food in all its glory.

A few years later, I opened Barlata, a tapas bar in Oakland, California. I liked northern California, but kept searching for another location in which to raise my family. While teaching at the Worlds of Flavor conference at the Culinary Institute of America in Napa, I met some people from the Central Market grocery store in Texas, and they asked me to come teach at their Central Market Cooking School. When I finally did and explored the city of Austin, it seemed like everything I was looking for: a modest-size, multicultural city open to all kinds of food and in need of a good Catalan restaurant. A few months later, a business opportunity came up, and I moved Barlata—and my entire family—to Austin, Texas.

In my restaurant, Barlata, and now in this book, I truly love sharing the food of my country. When I am asked for Catalan recipes, I have no problem giving them. My cooking doesn't invent anything dramatically new. Sure, I put my personal touches on the classic dishes, but the recipes here belong to Catalonia as much as they do to me. Take my *canelons* for example, a traditional celebration dish in and around Barcelona. I like to stuff *canelons* with beef brisket instead of more common Catalan meats like rabbit or pork because I came to love brisket after moving to Texas (see Brisket Canelones, page 192). My Shrimp, Scallop, and Octopus Ceviche (page 149) is another dish that isn't traditionally Catalan. But it is a bowl of tart and salty bar food that anyone from Catalonia to California can enjoy with a sip of chilled vermouth on a hot summer day.

Now I am called Executive Chef. The truth is, I'm still cooking the way my mama did when I was a boy . . . gathering the best local ingredients, preparing them simply, and infusing them with Catalan attitude. At its heart, Catalan cooking is down-to-earth home cooking, often done slowly while you relax and take care of other things around the house. Thankfully, the rest of the world can now experience true Catalan flavors with widely available ingredients like Marcona almonds and *pebre vernell* or pimentón (smoked paprika).

At this point, I've been living in America for more than half my life. But I never let go of Catalonia, and it will never let go of me. It is a magical place. Every year, I return to Vilafranca with my family and we continue to explore the extraordinary food in this corner of the world. We visit all the markets and eat everywhere—from little-known places on the beach to Michelin-starred restaurants in Barcelona—and I cook alongside the local chefs I've gotten to know over the years. I'm glad the rest of the world is starting to embrace the Catalan style of relaxed dining with small plates and communal tables. If you want to experience what it's like to eat in Catalonia at home, invite your friends over, make some *pica-pica* (page 37) a big paella (page 108), and tell everyone to dig in. Pass around the chilled vermouth, and after a few swigs, you'll begin to understand why Barcelona has become one of Europe's most popular cities. Food is our way of bringing people together. Catalonia is a food-lover's paradise, and whenever I go back I somehow learn how to squeeze even more deliciousness out of life. This time on the tour, I am happy to show you around.

CATALONIA THROUGH THE AGES

The food I share with you in this book has deep roots. Catalonia is a region of incredible gastronomical riches, and we Catalans are very proud of them. In fact, we have been fighting to keep others from claiming what is ours since the Middle Ages. For centuries, we have sought independence from other countries—even from Spain itself.

Catalonia sits in the northeast corner of Spain, separated from France and the rest of Europe by the majestic Pyrenees mountain range in the north. To the east, the Mediterranean Sea forms the Catalan coast around Barcelona and the Costa Brava. To the south and west sit the autonomous Spanish regions of Valencia and Aragon, respectively.

From the Pyrenees' icy snow to Barcelona's hot and sandy beaches, Catalonia has a huge range of climates. This small region is only about the size of New Hampshire yet produces an enormous diversity of flora and fauna. In the south, along the Ebro River delta, extensive plantations grow plump grains of Bahía, one of the preferred rice varieties for making paella. In the pine forests of the Pyrenees, you'll find more wild mushrooms and truffles than anywhere else in Spain, particularly our prized *rovellons*, meaty red-capped mushrooms my parents and I would forage every September. Beautiful alpine wildflowers dot the foothills, eaten by roaming goats, sheep, and cows, whose milk becomes the aromatic basis for some of Spain's most sought-after cheeses: earthy Garrotxa goat cheese; the intensely flavorful washed-rind sheep's milk cheese, Serrat; and Mató, an unsalted cow and goat's milk cheese dating back to medieval times. Back then and still today, this ricotta-like cheese is served with honey for a simple dessert called *Mel i Mató* (Honey and Mató Cheesecake, page 256).

Catalonia also lays claim to some of the oldest olive trees in Spain with Arbequina olives that yield extra-virgin oil heralded the world over for its buttery texture and intoxicating aromas. In the Penedès region, where I grew up, some of Spain's best wine grapes grow, such as xarello, important in our prize-winning cava sparkling wines.

I could go on and on about Catalonia's amazing seafood, its incredible variety of vegetables, and the Iberian pigs, which produce some of the world's finest salt-cured ham as well as unique sausages like *fuet* and *botifarra*, my personal weakness. But the story of Catalan cuisine is not just about its indigenous ingredients. It's also about war. Centuries of invasions, occupations, exploration, and trading have infused Catalan food with flavors as far-flung as Persian saffron and Oaxacan chocolate.

The ancient Phoenicians, Carthaginians, and Greeks were some of the earliest travelers to hit the Catalan shores around Barcelona. They traded with the native Celts and Iberians, particularly in salt, fish, and grapes,

and advanced the primitive local culture by introducing the potter's wheel and solid agricultural tools made of iron. They also introduced olives, almonds, chickpeas, and various grains, including wheat.

Around 200 BCE, the entire Iberian Peninsula (now Spain and Portugal) came under Roman rule. The Romans expanded existing agricultural irrigation with vast networks of aqueducts, canals, bridges, and roads, which increased food production and carried both trading goods and soldiers throughout the region. The Romans ruled Iberia for six hundred years, and the bread, cheese, wine, and olive oil produced from Catalonia's fertile soil enriched the lives of the Roman elite while also helping Roman armies to expand the empire all across Europe.

Many Romans eventually settled in Iberia, which they called Hispania. They cultivated and cooked with an assortment of beans, like favas and chickpeas, as well as chicories, chards, cabbages, radishes, and numerous fruits, such as apples, pears, dates, pomegranates, peaches, apricots, plums, cherries, lemons, and figs—in addition to nuts like hazelnuts, chestnuts, walnuts, and acorns. All of these foods are still key ingredients in Catalan cooking today.

In the fifth century, as the Roman Empire began to fall, the Germanic tribes collectively known as the Visigoths overtook Catalonia. Under them, the local gastronomy remained largely the same as it had been under Roman rule. That all changed in 711, when the Moors, mostly Arabs and Berbers from North Africa, crossed the straits of Gibraltar and gained control of Iberia. The Moors renamed the region al-Andalus and for hundreds of years afterward developed it into one of wealthiest countries in the Mediterranean region. The Moors improved Roman irrigation and fertilization systems,

lengthened the local growing seasons, and greatly increased agricultural production. They also improved pest control and perfected food preservation techniques. Muslim agricultural practices introduced a wide variety of plants and spices to the area, including artichokes, spinach, eggplants, carrots, caraway, bitter oranges, and sugar; and they expanded the region's use of spices like cinnamon, nutmeg, cloves, anise, and cumin. The Moors also brought hard durum wheat, which was ground into flour, mixed with water, and formed and dried into noodles that we still enjoy today as *fideus* (see Fideo Noodle Paella, page 133). Most important, the Moors revolutionized the manner in which Catalans eat. Instead of piling mounds of various foods on a single large platter, as was the custom inherited from the Romans, the Muslim scholar and gastronome named Ziryab popularized the trend of serving each type of food in succession on a separate plate, a practice that continues to this day in the way we enjoy tapas.

The Moors gradually succumbed to advancing Christian kingdoms all over Europe. By 1137, the Kingdom of Aragon came to power in Catalonia, and Barcelona was its main port of naval expansionism throughout the Mediterranean. Over the next several hundred years, Christian royals in the area grew incredibly wealthy from widespread trading. Their opulent courtly lifestyle led to sophisticated gastronomic feasts, and Catalan chefs became some of the most highly respected in Europe. During this time, in the fourteenth century, Spain's oldest cookbook, *Sent Soví*, was written in Catalan. It was a period of immense power and excess, and Catalonia's territories expanded southward to include Sardinia, Naples, and Sicily.

To unify control on the home front, Ferdinand of Aragon and Isabella of Castile were married in 1469. This political marriage was also a religious union—they were the "Catholic King and Queen." In the name of Catholicism, the Kingdom of Spain eventually began the Spanish Inquisition. Muslims and Jews who had inhabited Catalonia for centuries—and who had contributed significantly to its gastronomy—were pressured to convert to Christianity. What you ate could get you in trouble at that time: Food and politics were intertwined. Buying certain Moorish ingredients like eggplant, coriander, and saffron at a Catalan market could signal the presence of heretics in the neighborhood.

By 1492, the "reconquest" of Christian Spain from the Muslims was complete. Spanish explorers set out to conquer the Americas next. From then on, the nexus of Catalonia's commercial activity gradually shifted from the Mediterranean to the Atlantic. This economic shift ultimately resulted in Catalonia's decline as a European political power center.

The "Columbian Exchange," a period of massive trade in food, technology, people, and ideas in the fifteenth and sixteenth centuries, reshaped Catalonia's foodways yet again. Potatoes were brought from Peru, and Catalans made use of them in everything from *truita de patata i ceba* (Catalan Potato and Onion Omelet, page 55) to *patates braves* (Fried Potatoes with Spicy Tomato Sauce and Allioli, page 41). Tomatoes came from South and Central America, and Catalan cooks worked them into sauces such as the ubiquitous *sofregit* (page 34) and, most important, *pa amb tomàquet* (Catalan Tomato Bread, page 38), the foundation of every sandwich in Catalonia. Chile peppers of all kinds also arrived from Central and South America, and they became integral in our *pebre vernell* or pimentón (smoked paprika) and *romesco*

(Nut and Pepper Sauce, page 32). And to America, Catalans also owe a debt of gratitude for chocolate, the key flavor in our beloved afternoon treat of churros dipped in Spanish hot chocolate (page 240).

By the seventeenth century, Catalonia's gastronomy had become extremely diverse and sophisticated with influences from as far away as Paris, Persia, Palermo, and Peru. We Catalans were so proud of our cultural heritage that we sought independence from the Kingdom of Spain. At the time, Catalonia had a separate legal system, so we revolted against the kingdom's taxation policies. France got behind us in the fight, but King Philip V of Spain regained control of Catalonia in 1702. As punishment for the insurrection, Spanish royalty in Madrid completely abolished Catalan independence and forbade the Catalan language, a repression that would happen again in the future.

Between the mid-1800s and the early 1900s, massive industrialization helped Barcelona become the seat of Spain's economic power once again. By 1931, Spain had evolved into a democratic republic, and Catalonia had won its right to an autonomous government. Unfortunately, the Great Depression of the 1930s changed all that. Hard times threw the region into political and economic turmoil, and the conservative elite found their opening to regain control of the country. Right-wing Spanish Nationalist troops, led by Francisco Franco, staged a military coup. The ugly Spanish Civil War followed, and, despite left-wing liberals fighting hard for years, the resistance was gradually overcome and the stronghold of Barcelona fell to the Nationalists in 1939. From then until 1975, Francisco Franco ruthlessly ruled Spain as a military dictator. After winning the Civil War, the general's first step was to establish military

tribunals in order to lawfully imprison and execute thousands of resistors. Franco outlawed all unions and religions except Catholicism and banned the Catalan language once again.

I was born into and grew up under Franco's rule, and my Catalan culture, heritage, and cuisine were officially suppressed by the Spanish state. I always felt like an outsider in my own country. Politically, I was on the side of the Catalan resistance, and as a naive teenager, I participated in some risky rebellions. There were a few close calls with the military police—let's just say it's a good thing I came to America when I did! Catalonia is still fighting for its independence from Spain to this day.

Catalans are proud people. Despite the centuries of occupations and the decades of oppression, we have continued to develop our own food culture. After Franco's rule ended, Catalan cuisine became a major player on the world stage. One look at groundbreaking restaurants like Ferran Adrià's El Bulli and Joan Roca's El Celler de Can Roca will show you that.

Catalonia's complex history makes our culinary traditions especially sacred, something I have come to appreciate more and more as I have gotten older. I believe food and cooking form the backbone of every people around the world. My Catalan food culture was suppressed for so long that I take great pride in bringing my country's cuisine to you in this book. Through the recipes and stories here, I am thrilled to share the irresistible Catalan food and irrepressible Catalan spirit that lives and breathes in our bones.

ABOUT THIS BOOK

The recipes in this book came together from various people and places, including the Catalan tables of my childhood, meals enjoyed with family and friends over the years, and the kitchens of Catalan cooks I have come to respect and now consider colleagues despite the miles separating us.

The book starts off much like a Catalan meal with a group of *pica-pica*, or little bites of savory food. Then you'll find an assortment of vegetable and bean dishes—staples of our humble diet. I devote an entire chapter to *paelles*, other rice dishes, and *fideuà* (noodle dishes) because the diverse flavors in these grains express so much of our gastronomic history. From there, the region's main protein-based foods each have a chapter, including seafood, pork, and a special chapter called Del Corral ("From the Corral") including recipes made with chicken, duck, rabbit, lamb, and beef. Sweets are a not a huge part of home cooking in Catalonia, but I love them and included some of my favorites as well as a basic recipe for country-style bread.

Jump in and look around at the recipes to see what sparks your interest. I recommend starting with the little dishes, the *pica-pica*. These dishes are fairly easy to put together and will give you a good sense of Catalan flavors, especially if they are new to you. Paella is a bit more complex with multiple layers of flavor from the pounded garlic and sautéed rice to the rich stock, aromatic spices and herbs, and savory vegetables, meats, and seafood—not to mention the crispy bottom crust or *socarrat*. Dive into those recipes after you've tried a few of the others.

You'll notice some helpful notes within the recipes. These are called *El Consell*, which translates to something like "wise counsel" or "a word of advice." To help you cook like a Catalan, here are a few more things to keep in mind, including a handful of simple preparations you can make ahead of time and keep on hand so you're never too far away from a delicious meal.

COMPRANT
SHOPPING

Like all Catalans, I believe good cooking comes from good ingredients. Acquiring the freshest ingredients is often a daily ritual in Catalonia. Spanish home refrigerators tend to be small, so we have to buy fresh ingredients more frequently. When I grew up, there were no big supermarkets. We went to the fish store to find the freshest fish, to the butcher for the freshest meat, and to the bakery for fresh bread. Even though Barcelona has large markets today, you often find the best-quality ingredients at the specialty stores.

I recommend you do the same thing wherever you are: Shop small and seek out the real food specialists. Talk to your friends and neighbors to find the best fishmonger, butcher, and produce purveyor in the area. When you

find someone you like, ask them questions about where the food comes from and how it is grown. You may find yourself treated to special cuts reserved for only the best customers. For many Spanish ingredients outside of Spain, I shop at Hispanic grocery stores. I also order online, and a list of Spanish importers appears at the end of this book. When a suitable substitute for a traditional ingredient exists, I offer it in the recipe.

INGREDIENTES
INGREDIENTS

Many Catalan ingredients, including salt cod (page 156) and *botifarra* (page 203), are explained in detail in special features throughout the book. For specific paella ingredients, see "Tips for Perfect Paella," page 106. Here are some particulars on other ingredients frequently used in the recipes.

BLACK PEPPER: I don't always add black pepper to dishes. Sometimes it's not called for, especially when other peppers like fresh or dried chile peppers are already included in the dish. When I do season with black pepper, I like to grind it fresh and somewhat coarse.

BUTTER: Many of my recipes call for salted butter. That is my preference for savory cooking. For baking, I use unsalted.

CAVA VINEGAR: While sherry vinegar comes from the southern part of Spain, in Catalonia, we use cava vinegar made from cava, our unique sparkling white wine. If you can't find cava vinegar, use champagne vinegar. Either way, this type of vinegar is very subtle and mild, whereas sherry vinegar and red wine vinegar are very robust. Cava vinegar makes the perfect accompaniment to delicate dishes made with fish and vegetables.

EGGS: The recipes mostly call for large eggs, but one or two call for small eggs. If you only have large eggs, beat one large egg and pour out half to use as a small egg. I like to beat eggs thoroughly so the whites and yolks are completely blended. When making fresh egg preparations like omelets, I also prefer to use free-range or organic eggs; they just taste better.

GARLIC: Don't be tempted to buy pre-peeled cloves of garlic. They ferment and go bad quickly in the package. I also like to cut off the hard root end of the garlic clove before cutting the rest. If you happen to find a green sprout in your garlic clove, pull it out because it can taste bitter.

OIL: Growing up in Catalonia, all we had was extra-virgin olive oil, so that is mostly what I still use today. I love the taste of Arbequina olive oil. I may be biased because Arbequina is the predominant olive in Catalonia, but I love its thick texture and rich, mellow taste. It's not too pungent or aggressive, so it complements most foods. For salads, I use 100% extra-virgin olive oil. For sautéing, I usually mix 25% olive oil with 75% vegetable oil, such as canola or grapeseed. For deep-frying, I use 100% vegetable oil. I recommend you do the same.

ONIONS: After olive oil, onions are the most important ingredients in Catalan cooking. I often sweat them over low heat to coax out their complex flavors. When you take this technique to the extreme and cook them slowly for hours and hours, they caramelize and melt into a delicious, creamy Caramelized Onion Marmalade (page 29). I add these caramelized onions to various dishes for body and deep flavor notes. Don't be tempted to skip this preparation. Like the bass in jazz music, caramelized onions are what give many dishes their backbone. I call for yellow onions throughout the book, and they should be firm, plump, and juicy when you cut into them.

PEPPERS: Many fresh and dried peppers are popular in Catalan cooking, particularly fresh Holland bell peppers, which we love to roast until they are smoky and soft. We also roast deep green padrón peppers for snacking and blend up dried ñora chiles to make romesco sauce (page 32). If you can't find padróns, shishito peppers make a decent substitute. Anchos can stand in for ñoras, although anchos are a bit spicier. Since I live in Texas now—the land of chiliheads—I also use the occasional jalapeño, habanero, or cayenne-type pepper. Whatever fresh peppers you buy, be sure they are plump and juicy, rather than soft and mushy.

PIMENTÓN: Known in Catalan as *pebre vernell*, smoked chile pepper powder, a.k.a. smoked paprika, is one of the key flavors of Catalonia. There are many knockoffs out there now, so look for pimentón de La Vera, which is strictly regulated to ensure the peppers are smoked, dried, and ground in the region of La Vera, Spain. There are three types of pimentón: sweet, semi-spicy, and spicy. I only use sweet pimentón. If you can't find it, you can use Hungarian paprika as a last resort, but you'll miss the signature taste of woodsmoke.

SALT: I usually use two basic types of salt—kosher salt for cooking and flaky sea salt for finishing. I like the way these coarse salts feel between my fingers when I pick them up to season food. Sometimes when curing sausage or bacon, I'll use a tiny amount of pink salt (cure #1 or tinted cure mix), which is mostly sodium chloride with a minuscule amount of sodium nitrite to help prevent the growth of harmful bacteria. The recipes will always specify what type you need.

EINES
TOOLS FOR A CATALAN KITCHEN

Most of my recipes call for basic mixing bowls, sauté pans, saucepans, and skillets, including nonstick. But a well-stocked Catalan kitchen will also include a few special pieces of equipment.

CAST-IRON SKILLETS: Permanent instruments in my kitchen, cast-iron skillets never break, hold heat reliably, and can be used to make dozens of Catalan dishes. Sometimes I use a cast-iron skillet as a substitute for a paella pan—see the *rossejat* recipe (Roasted Rice Paella, page 122)—and it doubles as a serving dish for recipes like *gambes a l'ajillo* (Shrimp in Garlic Oil, page 59).

MORTAR AND PESTLE: A mortar is a heavy bowl—usually made of stone or ceramic—and is paired with a pestle. It is used to grind ingredients by smashing the pestle into the well of the bowl. Other than a sauté pan or paella pan, the mortar and pestle was the only piece of equipment I ever saw at home as a kid. It's how we would make Allioli (page 32) and crush hazelnuts or almonds for romesco (Nut and Pepper Sauce, page 32). To this day, I use a mortar and pestle for those tasks as well as for breaking apart grainy squid ink and grinding spices. This tool is absolutely necessary for Catalan cooking. Nothing compares to how a mortar and pestle crushes garlic. No matter how finely you mince garlic by hand or process it with a machine, you can't get the same result. You might be able to get away with an electric spice grinder for spices, but it is easier to control the fineness in a mortar. Look for a mortar with a wooden pestle. Someone might try to sell you a fancier one with both the mortar and pestle made of marble. Don't let them.

OILER: In Catalonia, every cook pours olive oil from a spouted bottle called a *setrill*, or oiler. The slender spout is especially helpful for slowly drizzling oil when making vinaigrette or *allioli*. A glass bottle fitted with a bartender's pouring spout also does the job.

PAELLA PAN: Catalans usually have a few different pans for different rice dishes. Deeper pans lend themselves to soupier rice dishes, which are simply called *arròs* (rice). But for paella, you want a wide, shallow pan to develop a large layer of crispy rice on the bottom. The term *paella* actually refers to the pan itself, and they are usually made of thin carbon steel to help develop the bottom layer of crispy rice called the *socarrat*. Paella

HOW TO CURE A PAELLA PAN

Curing a paella pan is much like curing or seasoning a cast-iron skillet and gives you some of the same nonstick properties. To cure a carbon steel pan, put it on the stovetop and fill it about three-quarters of the way with water. Add a few splashes of distilled white vinegar and boil the water over high heat until it reduces in volume by about half, about 10 minutes. This process removes the manufacturer's antirust coating. Dump out the water and dry the pan with a paper towel. Then use a clean paper towel to smear a thin layer of olive oil inside the pan. Sprinkle a layer of salt over the olive oil, then put the pan back over high heat until the oil starts smoking. The smoke means the oil is breaking down, which helps it bond with the metal, creating a nonstick surface and slight patina. Turn off the heat and let the pan cool on the stove. When it's cool, wipe out the salt, and then smear some fresh oil into the pan. Now it's ready. Clean the pan like you would a cast-iron pan. Scrub it with hot water but avoid using soap, which can remove the nonstick surface. After cleaning the pan, dry it thoroughly and, between uses, smear some fresh oil into the pan to keep it from rusting.

pans often need to be cured before using (see instructions, below left).

PLANXA: A *planxa* is a griddle—a very simple, very useful tool. A thick, heavy cast-iron griddle gives you a dark sear on octopus tentacles and heats evenly when cooking things like *cansalada* (Spanish bacon). If you don't have one, look for a heavy rectangular model so you have plenty of surface area to work with. A large cast-iron skillet can stand in for a planxa when necessary.

TORCH: You'll need a kitchen torch to make authentic *Crema Catalana* (Catalan Custard, page 246), the most famous dessert from our region. It's also helpful for making *carn crua* (Barlata Carpaccio, page 82), for which I briefly sear the surface of filet mignon. You can find an inexpensive kitchen torch at a restaurant supply store.

MISE EN PLACE
GETTING READY TO COOK

French for "put in place," mise en place is all about getting yourself organized before you start cooking. If you have everything in front of you, it makes the actual cooking so much more enjoyable. You don't want to be running around the kitchen looking for ingredients or equipment while your onions are burning on the stove. If it's your first time making a dish, read the recipe all the way through so you get a general idea of what you'll be doing. Get all your ingredients prepped and ready to go. Pull out any special utensils you may need. And keep your work area clear by cleaning as you go. Mise en place is important for all types of cooking, not just Catalan. But if Catalan cooking is new to you, it is especially important to have all of your ingredients and equipment in front of you before you start cooking. You'll get much better results that way.

RECEPTES BÀSIQUES

MAKE-AHEAD STAPLE RECIPES

Though simple, Catalan cooking is built on layers of flavor. When making dinner, my mother would reach into the pantry for a pinch of this, or she would open the refrigerator for a spoonful of that. Little did I know back then how important a pinch of adobo seasoning and a spoonful of caramelized onions were to her cooking! I know better now. Keep the following basic preparations in your kitchen (many can be stored frozen for weeks), and you'll always be ready to pull together a deeply flavored Catalan meal.

ADOB
ADOBO SEASONING

MAKES ABOUT ¼ CUP

1½ tablespoons pimentón (smoked paprika)

1 tablespoon kosher salt

½ teaspoon ground cumin

½ teaspoon sugar

½ teaspoon chili powder

½ teaspoon freshly grated nutmeg

½ teaspoon onion powder

½ teaspoon garlic powder

½ teaspoon freshly ground black pepper

¼ teaspoon cayenne pepper

Whisk all the ingredients together in a small airtight container, taking care to break apart any lumps. Cover and store at room temperature for up to 2 months.

EL CONSELL: It's quick and easy to mix up this seasoning blend and keep it on hand, but if you've run out, substitute store-bought adobo seasoning plus a generous pinch of pimentón.

SAL PER ALS ARROSSOS
PAELLA SALT

MAKES ABOUT ⅓ CUP

2 tablespoons kosher salt

2 tablespoons pimentón (smoked paprika)

1 tablespoon freshly ground black pepper

Whisk all the ingredients together in a small airtight container, taking care to break apart any lumps. Cover and store at room temperature for up to 2 months.

ALL CONFITAT
ROASTED GARLIC AND GARLIC OIL

MAKES 10 CLOVES GARLIC AND ABOUT ⅓ CUP OIL

10 garlic cloves (from about 1 medium head), peeled

¼ cup vegetable oil

2 tablespoons extra-virgin olive oil

1 Preheat the oven to 350°F.

2 Combine all the ingredients in a 6-ounce ramekin or small ovenproof bowl. Bake until the garlic is sizzling and golden brown, about 40 minutes. Remove the dish from the oven and let the garlic cloves cool completely in the oil, about 30 minutes. Using a slotted spoon, lift the garlic cloves from the oil and transfer them to an airtight container. Store refrigerated for up to 1 week. Pour the reserved oil into a small bottle, jar, or traditional *setrill* and store at room temperature for up to 1 week.

CEBA CONFITADA
CARAMELIZED ONION MARMALADE

MAKES ABOUT ⅓ CUP

2 tablespoons extra-virgin olive oil

2 tablespoons salted butter

2 medium yellow onions (about 1 pound), halved and thinly sliced

Kosher salt and freshly ground black pepper

1   In a large Dutch oven or heavy skillet, heat the oil and butter together over medium-low heat. When the butter is melted and foamy, add the onions and season with salt and pepper. Reduce the heat to low and cook, stirring occasionally to prevent burning, until the onions turn dark golden brown and sticky, 45 minutes to 1 hour. Be patient; don't turn up the heat.

2   When the onions are caramel brown, transfer them to a blender or food processor and pulse until smooth. Use immediately or store in an airtight container in the refrigerator for up to 3 days or in the freezer for up to 2 months.

EL CONSELL: It's hard to explain how important the flavor of caramelized onions can be in a dish. Even small amounts add deep flavors. If you only need a tiny amount for any recipe in this book, replace this marmalade with the onions already called for, then cook them in the pan used for the recipe. Instead of a quick, hot sauté, cook the onions slowly in a little oil over low heat until they become deep, dark brown in color, 30 to 45 minutes (depending on the total volume of onions), and then continue with the rest of the dish. Slow-cooking coaxes the most complex sweetness from the onions. If the onions threaten to burn over the long cooking time, stir in a splash of water.

PICADA
POUNDED GARLIC AND PARSLEY

MAKES ABOUT ⅓ CUP

6 to 8 medium garlic cloves, roughly chopped

1 teaspoon kosher salt

3 cups fresh curly parsley leaves (discard small stems)

¼ cup extra-virgin olive oil

1   Mash the garlic and salt together in a mortar with a pestle until the garlic is completely broken into a fine paste. Add the parsley leaves gradually in small pinches, smashing them completely before adding more. The herbs will go from looking fluffy to dark green and wet to a green paste. It takes a long time; salt helps. So do friends. Stir in the olive oil.

2   To store, spoon the picada into ice cube trays in 1-tablespoon portions and pour a thin layer of oil on top of each portion. Freeze until solid. Transfer the frozen picada portions to a freezer bag, squeeze out the air, and seal. Store in the freezer for up to 3 months. Thaw before using or add directly to the pan for dishes that will be simmering.

EL CONSELL: Catalans use picada to flavor many different paelles, to thicken various stews, and to drizzle over rice dishes. The importance of picada in Catalan cooking cannot be overstated. It is a general term for a mashed sauce, traditionally pounded together in a mortar and pestle. I have incorporated different versions of picada into many of the recipes in this book, but you could use this picada as a shortcut whenever pounded garlic, parsley, olive oil, and salt are called for in the recipe.

ALLIOLI
AIOLI

MAKES ABOUT ½ CUP

2 garlic cloves, smashed
Pinch of kosher salt
6 tablespoons vegetable oil
2 tablespoons extra-virgin olive oil
1 large egg yolk
½ teaspoon red wine vinegar

1 Mash the smashed garlic and salt together in a mortar with a pestle until the garlic is completely broken into a fine paste. Combine the oils in a spouted measuring cup.

2 Scrape the garlic paste into a medium bowl. Whisk in the egg yolk until the yolk is loose and a bit pale. Whisking constantly, begin adding the blended oil a few drops at a time. Be sure each drop is fully whisked in before adding the next. As the base thickens, you can add oil a bit faster down the side of the bowl in a steady trickle, continuing to whisk constantly. When thickened, begin whisking in the vinegar. The allioli is finished when all the oil and vinegar is whisked in and the mixture is white or pale yellow, shiny, and stands up firm like Greek yogurt. Add a drop or two of water if it is too thick, and season with more salt if needed.

3 Spoon the allioli into an airtight container, cover the surface with plastic wrap, and store in the refrigerator for 1 to 2 days.

EL CONSELL: Strictly traditional allioli uses about four times as much garlic as this recipe and skips the egg yolk. But I like how the yolk mellows out the garlic a bit and keeps the sauce smooth and creamy.

In a "broken" allioli, the oil will separate out from everything else and the mixture will look lumpy. If this happens, whisk a single egg yolk in a medium bowl until the yolk is pale yellow. Then whisk or blend in the broken allioli in a slow, steady trickle. It will re-emulsify, regaining its smooth texture.

If you're in a real pinch, you could cheat by mixing the mashed garlic into store-bought mayonnaise.

ROMESCO
NUT AND PEPPER SAUCE

MAKES ABOUT 1 CUP

2 dried ñora chiles or 1 ancho chile
1 cup boiling water
⅓ cup skin-on almonds
2 Roma or vine tomatoes
¼ cup plus 2 tablespoons extra-virgin olive oil
2 slices stale bread, crusts removed
6 garlic cloves, peeled and whole
Kosher salt
Small pinch of crushed red pepper (optional; see note)
1 tablespoon red wine vinegar

1 Position one rack 4 to 6 inches from the broiler and another rack in the center of the oven. Preheat the oven to 350°F.

2 Place the dried chiles in a small heatproof bowl and pour the boiling water over them. Let stand until the chiles swell significantly and soften, about 15 minutes. Drain. Remove the stems and seeds from the chiles and set the flesh aside.

3 Meanwhile, arrange the almonds in a single layer on a sheet pan and bake in the center of the oven until fragrant and toasted, about

10 minutes. Remove from the oven and set aside.

4   Turn the oven to broil. Place the tomatoes on a sheet pan and broil until blackened all over, about 5 minutes, turning once or twice. Transfer to a small heatproof bowl and cover with plastic wrap. Let stand until cool enough to handle, about 5 minutes. Remove the skins from the tomatoes and set aside.

5   In a medium saucepan, heat ¼ cup of the oil over medium-high heat. When the oil is shimmering, add the bread and toast until it is golden brown and crisp, about 2 minutes. Remove to a plate. Add the garlic to the hot oil and cook, stirring, until the garlic is golden brown, about 3 minutes. Remove the pan from the heat.

6   Mash the softened chiles with a pinch of salt in a mortar with a pestle until all the skin is broken down. (You can also do this in a processor, but the color and texture will be slightly different. Add the ingredients in the order specified.) Break the bread into little pieces and add to the mortar or processor, then pound or process the bread to break it apart. Add the almonds, garlic, and pepper flakes and pound or process well after each addition, until the mixture forms a buttery paste. Pound or pulse in the charred tomatoes until smooth, occasionally scooping the corners of the mortar with a spoon or scraping down the sides of the processor bowl to draw in the ingredients. Stir or pulse in the vinegar, remaining 2 tablespoons oil, and a few generous pinches of salt.

7   Store in an airtight container in the refrigerator for up to 1 week. Or spoon the romesco into ice cube trays in 2-tablespoon portions. Pour a thin layer of oil on top of each cube. Freeze until solid and then transfer the frozen romesco to freezer bags, squeeze out all the air, and seal. Store in the freezer for up to 3 months. Thaw before using or add directly to the pan for dishes that will be simmering.

EL CONSELL: Skip the red pepper flakes if you use ancho chiles. The anchos will be spicy enough.

SOFREGIT
SOFRITO

MAKES ABOUT 1½ CUPS

⅓ cup extra-virgin olive oil
1 medium yellow onion, finely chopped
A few generous pinches of kosher salt
1 small green bell pepper, finely chopped
1 can (15 ounces) tomato sauce

1   In a medium saucepan, heat the oil over medium-high heat. When the oil is shimmering, add the onion and salt, and reduce the heat to medium-low. Cook until the onion is translucent, about 15 minutes, stirring often to prevent burning. Stir in the bell pepper and cook until the onion is pale golden and very soft and the pepper is tender, about 15 minutes more. When it is ready, the onion will fall apart in your fingers. Give it time.

2   Add the tomato sauce, increase the heat to medium-high, and bring to a boil. Reduce the heat to low and simmer gently for 1½ hours, stirring occasionally. You should see only a few bubbles here and there as the sauce cooks. The sofregit is finished when it concentrates to a thick, chunky texture and falls from a spoon in one dollop.

3   To store, spoon the sofregit into ice cube trays in 2-tablespoon portions. Freeze until solid, then transfer to freezer bags, squeeze out all the air, and seal. Store for up to 3 months. Thaw before using or add directly to the pan for dishes that will be simmering.

EL CONSELL: In Spanish, *sofreír* (*sofregir* in Catalan) means to cook slowly, and slowly cooking onions is the most important step to a deeply flavored sofregit. Take your time.

You could use fresh tomatoes here, but the truth is I've had the best results with a can of smooth tomato sauce (not Italian pasta sauce). Look for tomato sauce (or pureed and strained tomatoes) near the other canned tomato products in your market. In a pinch, you could substitute good-quality store-bought Spanish sofrito from a market such as La Tienda.

BROU DE POLLASTRE, CARN, O VERDURES
CHICKEN, BEEF, PORK, VEAL, OR VEGETABLE STOCK

MAKES ABOUT 4 QUARTS

½ pound beef, veal, pork, or chicken bones, rinsed with cold water and patted dry

1 small carrot, peeled and roughly chopped

2 celery ribs, roughly chopped

1 large yellow onion, peeled and quartered

1½ teaspoons black peppercorns

1 bay leaf

1 Preheat the oven to 350°F.

2 Arrange the bones with the carrot, celery, and onion in a large roasting pan or on a sheet pan, and roast until evenly browned, 30 to 45 minutes, shaking the pan occasionally.

3 Transfer the pan contents to a large stockpot. Add the peppercorns, bay leaf, and enough water to cover the ingredients (about 1 gallon). Bring to a simmer over high heat, then reduce the heat to low so the water barely simmers. Simmer gently for 2 hours, skimming off any fat or froth occasionally.

4 Place a fine-mesh strainer over a large bowl. Pour the stock through the strainer and use a pestle or wooden spoon to press all the liquid from the solids (discard the solids). Set the stock aside to cool.

5 Transfer the stock to the refrigerator to chill completely, then divide it into airtight containers. Cover and store in the refrigerator for up to 1 week or in the freezer for up to 3 months.

EL CONSELL: This recipe can be adapted to make vegetable stock. Just skip the bones and roast another onion, carrot, and celery rib.

FUMET DE PEIX
FISH STOCK

MAKES ABOUT 4 QUARTS

1 cup dry white wine

1 pound white fish bones, rinsed and halved if large

1 small yellow onion, peeled and halved

1 fennel stalk (upper light green part), roughly chopped

1 celery rib, roughly chopped

1 Roma or vine tomato, halved

¼ teaspoon black peppercorns

3 bay leaves

1 In a large stockpot, combine the wine, bones, onion, fennel, celery, tomato, peppercorns, and bay leaves and add 1 gallon water. Bring to a simmer over high heat, then reduce the heat to low so the liquid barely simmers. Cook until the stock is flavorful and pale gold in color, about 1 hour, skimming off the froth occasionally.

2 Place a fine-mesh strainer over a large bowl. Pour the stock through the strainer and use a pestle or wooden spoon to press all the liquid from the solids (discard the solids). Set the stock aside to cool.

3 Transfer the stock to the refrigerator to chill completely, then divide into airtight containers. Cover and store in the refrigerator for up to 1 week or in the freezer for up to 3 months.

EL CONSELL: Ask your fishmonger for extra spines, collars, heads, ribs, and tails of mild white fish such as red snapper.

PICA-PICA
LITTLE BITES

Catalans eat and drink well as a way of life. It's all about the hospitality, the company at your table, and the quality of the food. Nothing is more important than those unique shared moments over little bites of good food and conversation. Our food culture has evolved to nurture these special moments so they can occur everywhere from tapas bars to *chiringuitos* (beachside restaurants) to *fondes* (inns serving food).

PA AMB TOMÀQUET

CATALAN TOMATO BREAD

Pa amb tomàquet is the foundation of every sandwich in Catalonia. If the smear of tomato is missing, it gets sent back to the kitchen. Though it can be topped with a variety of tasty sausages or tinned fish, the basic recipe is difficult to improve. Look for ripe and soft tomatoes that have been stored only at room temperature. The proper bread will have a crisp crust. You also don't want the loaf to be too tall (about 2 inches tall at most) because you will halve the entire loaf horizontally so the crust is on either side. If you're making this recipe for a crowd, grate the pulp from halved tomatoes, then use a spoon to spread it onto the toasts. It goes faster that way and the bread won't be soggy by the time you're ready to serve it.

1 round or long loaf crispy bread, such as ciabatta

2 to 3 garlic cloves, peeled and halved

2 to 3 ripe small vine tomatoes, halved crosswise

Extra-virgin olive oil

Flaky sea salt

1   Slice the bread in half horizontally, as if for a sandwich. Cut the bread halves crosswise into rectangles or squares, 4 to 5 inches in diameter, and toast them in a toaster or toaster oven until golden brown, 2 to 3 minutes. You can also toast them under the broiler or on a grill for 1 to 2 minutes per side.

2   Gently rub the cut sides of the garlic cloves all over the crispy sides of the toast. Then rub the cut sides of the tomatoes over the toast until the tomato pulp falls apart and seeps into the nooks and crannies. When the tomato halves have given up all their pulp and are completely spent, discard the remaining tomato skins and cores. Be sure the tomato pulp is spread evenly to all corners of the bread.

3   Drizzle the toast with a generous amount of olive oil, then sprinkle with salt. Sometimes I like to press the oily sides of the toasts together to help squeeze the oil deep into the toast. You can also cut each toast square on a diagonal to make triangles.

EL CONSELL: To make this dish more special, add a drizzle of Pimentón Oil (page 147) just before serving.

PATATES BRAVES

FRIED POTATOES WITH SPICY TOMATO SAUCE AND ALLIOLI

SERVES 4
GENEROUSLY

I am very proud of these *patates braves*. I believe they are at least as good as, if not better than, any I've tasted in Spain. The cut potatoes are boiled and then fried in small batches so they are perfectly crisp. After boiling, the potatoes need to chill for a few hours, so start making them the morning before you plan to serve them, or even the night before. I like to serve them in a small bowl with flavorful braves sauce (a spicy sofrito), a large spoonful of allioli, and a drizzle of pimentón oil. This very popular tapa is one I crave with a cold beer in my hand.

Kosher salt

4 medium russet potatoes (about 2 pounds), peeled and cut into 1-inch cubes

½ small habanero chile

½ small red onion

¾ cup Sofregit (page 34) or store-bought sofrito

About 6 cups vegetable oil, for deep-frying

1 teaspoon Adobo Seasoning (page 28) or store-bought adobo

A generous pinch of pimentón (smoked paprika)

½ cup Allioli (page 32) or store-bought aioli, for serving

1   Bring a large pot of water to a boil over high heat. Salt the water.

2   When the water is boiling, add the potatoes and cook until they are knife-tender, about 15 minutes. Drain the potatoes and arrange them in a single layer on a sheet pan until they are cool enough to handle. Remove the cooled potatoes from the sheet pan and transfer them to the refrigerator to chill for at least 4 to 5 hours or up to 3 days.

3   To make the braves pepper sauce, in a blender or food processor, combine the habanero, onion, and sofregit and pulse until very smooth. Transfer the puree to a small saucepan and cook slowly over low heat until the flavors blend and the sauce thickens slightly, 8 to 10 minutes.

4   Heat 2 inches of vegetable oil in a large Dutch oven over medium heat to 350°F. Adjust the heat as necessary to maintain the 350°F frying temperature. Working in batches, add the potatoes and fry, flipping the potatoes occasionally, until they are golden brown all over and very crisp, 4 to 6 minutes per batch. Transfer the potatoes to a large metal bowl. Immediately add the adobo seasoning and pimentón to the hot potatoes and toss to coat. Serve the potatoes in a medium bowl topped with the braves pepper sauce and allioli.

ANEM AL BAR

CATALAN BAR CULTURE

In Catalonia, the experience of tapas is a festivity. You go to a bar or restaurant, sit at a table with friends, and order a variety of small plates to be passed around. As the night goes on, everyone shares their favorite foods, orders a few more plates, and excitement builds at the table. It's no secret that Catalans like to drink. For us, leisure time and work time are equally important. We spend many hours socializing in bars, and tapas are a natural extension of our proclivity for drink. *Tapa* actually means "lid" and refers to the way Catalans perch small plates of food on top of their drinks. We love small bites of food with our drinks so much that we have several words describing different types of tapas. *Pica-pica* means "pinch pinch." These are even smaller snacks usually served as single bites. *Pinxos* are skewered foods, and they are typically on full display on the countertop of the bar like a buffet from which guests can pick and choose.

A meal of tapas is like having a tasting menu of your own creation without any pretense: It's greasy fingers holding on to a cold beer; piles of mussel shells and crumpled napkins; and pimentón oil sopped up from a plate of seared octopus with crisp bread smeared with tomato and garlic. It's a hunger and mess best understood in the aftermath: a jumbled table strewn with empty wineglasses and small plates licked clean.

Outside of Catalonia, you can reproduce the food reasonably well. But the hard part is re-creating the experience. The *attitude* toward eating is different in other countries and, as a result, less fluid and less exploratory. In Catalonia, a meal of tapas turns dining into a special event to be entered into with abandon and shared with everyone at the table. Nowhere else could be better or more important than where you are—except maybe the next tapas bar down the street!

LLISTAT DE PREUS:
- ARENGADES FUMADES 30,€/KG.
- BOQUERONS 30.€/KG.
- ANXOVES FILET 0,80 u.
- CEBETES AGREDOLCES 20,€/KG.
- PEBROT FARCIT FORMATGE 35,€/KG.
- PEBROT FARCIT TONYINA 35,€/KG.
- ENVOLTINI TOMAQUET 35,€/KG.
- CARXOFES BRASA 35,€/KG.
- TOMAQUET SEC AMB OLI 25,€/KG.
- DOLMADES 0,50 u.
- BANDERILLAS BOQUERONS 0,75€/u.
- CARPACCIO BACALLA 55,€/KG.
- PEBROT MORRO 8,€/KG.
- COGOMBRES AMB VINAGRE 5,-€/KG.
- LLOMS SARDINES "FUMADES" 1,50 pega
- BONITOL AMB OLI 25,95€/KG.
- BONITOL AMB ESCABETX 25,95
- LLOMS DE SALMÓ 49,- €/KG.

PEBROTS A LA BRASA

GRILLED PADRÓN OR SHISHITO PEPPERS

SERVES 4

I like to grill these peppers without oil so they char instead of caramelize. After grilling, a little adobo seasoning, a drizzle of extra-virgin olive oil, and a squeeze of lemon are all they need. In Catalonia, you'll see grilled padrón peppers served at most tapas bars, but padróns can be hard to find outside of Catalonia year-round. Shishito peppers are similar in size, shape, and flavor and make a good substitute, though they tend to be slightly milder.

½ pound padrón or shishito peppers, rinsed and dried well

2 tablespoons extra-virgin olive oil

½ teaspoon Adobo Seasoning (page 28) or store-bought adobo

Flaky sea salt, for serving

4 lemon wedges, for serving

Preheat a grill or grill pan to high. Grill the peppers until they blister and char in spots, about 5 minutes. Remove the peppers to a large bowl, add the oil and adobo, and toss to coat. Sprinkle with sea salt and serve with lemon wedges alongside for squeezing.

HOW TO FILLET FRESH ANCHOVIES

Hold the fish under running water over a
medium bowl to catch the discarded bits.
Using the dull side of a paring knife, scrape
away the scales from the body, working from
head to tail. Place your fingers below the gills
and snap off the head, pulling out the innards
with it. Use a paring knife to slit the belly and
rinse out any remaining innards. The fish will
naturally begin to butterfly, and you will see a
fillet on both sides of the belly. Flatten the fish
with your fingers until it is fully butterflied. Lift
the tail to pull the backbone away from the
flesh, discarding the backbone. Slice or pinch
off the top fin and tail of the fish.

SEITONS
PICKLED ANCHOVIES

Fresh anchovies are very hard to come by outside of Spain. I tend to save this recipe for trips home in the summer, where it's easy to find them. If you can get your hands on these small fish (beg your favorite fishmonger or even try a bait shop near a fishing town), this recipe is incredibly simple and worth making. The key is recognizing the freshness of the fish: They should smell clean like the ocean and not "fishy." The skins should be firm and shiny, particularly around the bellies. Even though *boquerones*—the Spanish name for this pickled preparation of anchovies—hail from Santander in Spain, we Catalans love them, too. We just prefer to call them *seitons*.

1 cup red wine vinegar

1 teaspoon kosher salt

12 ounces fresh anchovies, filleted (see opposite)

1 cup extra-virgin olive oil, plus more as needed

1 tablespoon finely chopped fresh curly parsley

1 tablespoon finely chopped garlic

1   In a medium shallow dish (big enough to hold the fillets in a single layer), combine 1 cup water and the vinegar. Stir in the salt. Layer the filleted anchovies on the bottom of the dish, skin-side down. Set aside until the fish flesh turns white, about 1 hour.

2   Drizzle a layer of oil over the bottom of a small glass dish just big enough to hold all of the anchovies comfortably. Removing the anchovies from the vinegar mixture one at a time, and allowing the excess liquid to drip off, make a layer of fish in the smaller dish. Drizzle the fish with more oil, then scatter on a pinch each of parsley and garlic. Repeat the layering until all have been used up. Add enough oil to cover the anchovies completely. Cover the dish and refrigerate for at least 3 hours before serving. Seitons will keep up to 1 week; as you use them, be sure the remaining anchovies are covered in oil.

EL CONSELL: In Catalonia, we eat seitons with nothing but chilled vermouth. You could also serve them with sliced pears and Idiazabal cheese.

ESQUEIXADA

SHREDDED SALT COD SALAD
WITH TOMATOES AND OLIVES

SERVES 4

In Catalonia—or really anywhere—this salt cod salad is perfect for summer when the days are hot and the tomatoes are ripest. It is best served on cold plates, as the plates chill the ingredients, making everything taste more refreshing. Sometimes I scatter thinly sliced Pickled Red Onions (page 212) on the salad for a twist on the classic dish.

½ pound salt cod, desalted (see page 157) and drained

4 tomatoes (about 1 pound), such as large Roma or vine tomatoes, halved crosswise

1 tablespoon sherry vinegar

3 tablespoons extra-virgin olive oil, plus more for serving

Kosher salt and freshly ground black pepper

Flaky sea salt, such as Maldon, for serving

12 pitted oil-cured olives, halved lengthwise

1 tablespoon chopped fresh curly parsley, for serving

1   Chill four salad plates until they are cold, at least 30 minutes.

2   Tear the cod into bite-size pieces with your fingers. Finely chop and set aside.

3   Grate the cut sides of the tomatoes on the large holes of a box grater. Stop grating when you reach the skin and most of the tomato pulp has been grated. You should have about 1¼ cups tomato pulp.

4   In a medium bowl, whisk together the vinegar and oil with a generous pinch each of kosher salt and pepper.

5   To serve, spoon about ¼ cup of tomato pulp onto each chilled plate and sprinkle with flaky sea salt. Divide the cod among the plates and spoon on the remaining tomato pulp and the olives. Spoon the vinaigrette over the salad, sprinkle with the parsley and a touch more sea salt, and drizzle with additional olive oil, if desired.

CROQUETES D'IBÈRIC
IBÉRICO HAM CROQUETTES

Croquetes are meant to be crunchy on the outside and soft on the inside. They are held together with a thick béchamel sauce and, for the crust, rolled in flour, egg, and breadcrumbs. To get the texture right, the filling chills for 3 hours before cooking, so start these ahead of time or even the night before. While Ibérico ham is expensive, if you happen to have trimmings left over from carving an entire leg, the leftover bits are perfect to use in this dish. The carved leg bone also steeps in the milk used for the béchamel, deepening its savory flavor. If you can't get Ibérico ham, use Serrano, which is less expensive and more widely available.

FILLING
4 tablespoons (½ stick) salted butter

1 medium onion, finely chopped

½ cup all-purpose flour

2 cups whole milk

6 ounces Ibérico ham or Serrano ham, finely chopped

1 to 2 teaspoons kosher salt

SAUCE
1 cup Sofregit (page 34) or store-bought sofrito

½ tablespoon minced roasted red pepper

½ tablespoon extra-virgin olive oil

3 cloves Roasted Garlic (page 28)

¼ teaspoon ground cumin

Kosher salt

ASSEMBLY
½ cup all-purpose flour, plus more for sprinkling

2 large eggs, lightly beaten

1 cup fine breadcrumbs

6 cups vegetable oil, for deep-frying

1   Make the filling: In a medium saucepan, melt the butter over medium-high heat. Add the onion, reduce the heat to medium-low, and cook slowly until the onions are translucent, about 15 minutes, stirring often.

2   Whisk in ½ cup of the flour (it will grab on to the onions and make a thin film at the bottom of the pan) and cook until the flour is lightly toasted, about 3 minutes. Gradually add the milk, whisking constantly, until the mixture is smooth. Simmer and stir until it becomes very thick, like porridge. Stir in the chopped ham and then taste the mixture, adding salt until it tastes good to you.

3   Line a 13 × 9-inch baking pan with plastic wrap. Scrape the milk mixture onto the pan and let cool to room temperature, about 1 hour. Press plastic wrap onto the surface of the mixture, sealing the edges, and transfer the pan to the refrigerator to chill thoroughly, about 3 hours or overnight. The filling will firm up to a soft dough.

(recipe continues)

4   Make the sauce: In a blender or food processor, combine the sofregit, roasted red pepper, olive oil, garlic, and cumin and process until smooth. Season with a pinch of salt and transfer the sauce to a medium saucepan. Cook over medium heat until warmed through, about 5 minutes.

5   Assemble the croquetes: Use a large spoon to portion the chilled filling into 1-ounce pieces (about 2 tablespoons). Roll the pieces into small, thick cylinders. If the filling is too soft to handle, sprinkle in just enough flour to keep it from sticking to your hands. Place the rolled croquetes on a sheet pan as you form them.

6   Set up three shallow bowls for dredging: Place the ½ cup flour in one bowl, the eggs in a second, and the breadcrumbs in the third. Dip each *croqueta* in the flour, then egg, then breadcrumbs, coating thoroughly with each dip. Set on a wire rack as they are coated.

7   Heat the vegetable oil in a medium Dutch oven over medium heat to 350°F. Adjust the heat as necessary to maintain the 350°F frying temperature. Working in batches, gently add the croquetes and fry until they are evenly crisp and dark golden brown, 3 to 5 minutes, turning occasionally with tongs.

8   Serve the croquetes hot alongside a bowl of warm sofregit sauce for dipping.

EL CONSELL: Croquetes can be difficult to handle. To shape them consistently, put the filling into a pastry bag fitted with a 24mm (½ inch) round tip, and pipe a long log the thickness of your thumb. Cut the log crosswise into croquetes about 2 inches long. To make these ahead, you can freeze the croquetes before breading them. Arrange the shaped croquetes on a large sheet pan or a 13 × 9-inch baking pan lined with freezer or parchment paper. Transfer the pan to the freezer until the croquetes are solid, about 1 hour. Then transfer the frozen croquetes to a resealable bag labeled with the date. Use within 3 months and thaw slightly before breading and frying as directed.

POTATO CHIP OMELET

One morning, desperate for a truita but feeling lazy, I discovered a surprising hangover cure: a bag of potato chips. Using cooked potato chips saves about a half hour of cook time. While the sweated onions are still in the pan, just finely crush enough handfuls of potato chips to fill the pan three-quarters of the way. An 8-ounce bag of chips works nicely—I like the thicker chips kettle-cooked in olive oil. Let the chips soak up the liquid from the onion to soften them. Stir the crushed chips and onions into the egg mixture while the chip mixture is still warm, then cook the eggs as directed.

TRUITA DE PATATA I CEBA
CATALAN POTATO AND ONION OMELET

This traditional omelet recipe has as many variations as paella and is almost as beloved by Catalans. There are two secrets to a successful truita: Sweat the onions slowly without browning them, and use a nonstick skillet. The potatoes could be diced or shaved and the dish would still be considered authentic, but undercooked or overcooked onions would make the dish unrecognizable. The eggs are separated and their whites are beaten with a fork to fluff them up and create a light and soft truita. With a dollop of Allioli (page 32) and a piece of Catalan Tomato Bread (page 38), this dish brings joy to my family on a weekly basis.

½ cup extra-virgin olive oil

2 small yellow onions, finely chopped

2 teaspoons kosher salt

2 medium russet potatoes (about 1 pound), peeled and cut into ½-inch cubes

½ teaspoon freshly ground black pepper

6 large eggs, separated

1   Preheat the oven to 300°F.

2   In a medium ovenproof nonstick skillet, heat about half the oil over medium heat. When the oil is shimmering, stir in the onions and salt. Reduce the heat to low, cover, and sweat the onions until they release liquid, becoming soft and translucent, about 15 minutes. Stir the potatoes into the onions (the pan will be quite full). Cook, covered, until the potatoes are soft but still hold their shape, 20 to 25 minutes, stirring occasionally. Stir in the pepper.

3   Place the egg whites in a large bowl and the yolks in a small bowl. Use a whisk or fork to beat the egg whites until foamy, then beat the yolks into the whites. The mixture should be pale orange or yellow with bubbles on top.

4   Stir the potato and onion mixture into the frothy eggs. The mixture will thicken slightly. Wipe the skillet clean with a paper towel, then return it to medium heat and add the remaining oil. When the oil is shimmering, pour in the egg mixture and use a silicone spatula to spread the ingredients in an even layer. Cook until the top is firm except for a thin pool of custard in the center, about 10 minutes, shaking the pan occasionally to redistribute any uncooked egg.

5   Transfer the skillet to the oven and bake until the egg is firm yet moist and springs back a little when touched, 12 to 18 minutes, rotating the pan once or twice for even cooking. Place a large plate over the top of the skillet and carefully invert the skillet to release the *truita*.

BUNYOLS DE BACALLÀ
SALT COD FRITTERS

Everyone's grandmother makes *bunyols de bacallà* differently, and everyone has an opinion about what makes the best version. Some cooks swear by bunyols with a choux pastry base and others prefer potato. Here is my favorite—a combination of choux pastry and potato—made with some help from a friend and top chef in Barcelona, Jordi Vila. This is a fritter with salt cod in it, sort of like an American hush puppy flecked with parsley and garlic and still soft on the inside. It's my favorite because the texture is so light. To get a jump on things, soak the cod the day before assembling and cooking the fritters. After you mix the batter, it also helps to let it sit a few hours to create a creamier texture.

1 medium to large russet potato (about 10 ounces), peeled and cut into 1- to 2-inch pieces

½ pound salt cod, desalted (see page 157), drained, and cut into 1- to 2-inch pieces

1 tablespoon lard

1 tablespoon salted butter

1 cup all-purpose flour

2 large eggs

3 garlic cloves, finely chopped

2 tablespoons finely chopped fresh curly parsley

½ teaspoon kosher salt

6 cups vegetable oil, for deep-frying

1 cup Allioli (page 32) or store-bought aioli, for serving

1   Bring a large pot of water to a boil over high heat. Add the potatoes and boil until very tender, about 15 minutes. Use a slotted spoon to transfer the potatoes to a medium bowl, reserving the water in the pot. Return the water to a boil over high heat. Meanwhile, mash the potatoes using a fork or potato masher.

2   Add the salt cod to the boiling water, reduce the heat to medium, and simmer until the cod is soft and easy to shred, about 2 minutes. Reserving ½ cup of the cooking water, drain the salt cod. Shred the salt cod into small pieces using a fork or your fingers. Stir the lard and butter into the reserved water until melted, about 1 minute.

3   Spoon the flour into a stand mixer fitted with the whisk attachment. With the mixer running on low, slowly add the warm water mixture in a thin, steady stream. Add the eggs one at a time, mixing well after each addition.

4   Stir the salt cod, garlic, parsley, and salt into the mashed potatoes. Beat the potato mixture into the dough. Cover the dough and set aside to rest for 3 hours to allow the dough to cool and thicken.

5   Heat the vegetable oil in a medium Dutch oven over medium heat to 375°F. Adjust the heat as necessary to maintain the 375°F frying temperature. Use a 1-ounce (2-tablespoon) cookie scoop or a good eye and a spoon to portion the bunyols into pieces about 1½ inches in diameter. Drop the pieces directly into the hot oil as you portion them. Cook the bunyols in batches until they are crisp and golden brown all over and cooked through, about 2 minutes per batch, turning with tongs. Transfer to paper towels to drain.

6   Serve the bunyols warm with allioli alongside for dipping.

EL CONSELL: The secret to tender and flavorful bunyols is to give the dough a nap before frying the fritters. I like a 3-hour nap. Don't rush or skip it. The batter will cool to room temperature and become thicker as the flavors permeate.

GAMBES A L'AJILLO

SHRIMP IN GARLIC OIL

My deepest memories come from playing around in the kitchen as a boy while my mother cooked. The savory aroma of sofregit and the smell of frying garlic always remind me of her, as do the smells in this dish. I like to serve it to guests in small cast-iron skillets with the shrimp and garlic still sizzling. The aromas of garlic and oil waft up from the pan, engulfing your senses.

4 teaspoons vegetable oil

2 teaspoons extra-virgin olive oil

4 medium garlic cloves, thinly sliced

8 medium tail-on shrimp (21/25 count), peeled and deveined

½ teaspoon Adobo Seasoning (page 28) or store-bought adobo, plus a generous pinch of pimentón (smoked paprika)

1 tablespoon finely chopped fresh curly parsley, for serving

1   In a cold 6-inch cast-iron skillet, stir together the oils and garlic. Tuck the shrimp together in a single layer on top. Place the skillet over medium-high heat and sprinkle a generous pinch (about ¼ teaspoon) of adobo seasoning over the shrimp as they begin to sizzle. Sear the shrimp until they are pink on one side, about 2 minutes, shaking the pan once or twice to keep the garlic from burning. Use tongs to turn the shrimp and cook until they are bright pink, about 1 minute more.

2   Sprinkle with the remaining adobo seasoning and remove the skillet from the heat. Let stand for about 30 seconds, garnish with parsley, and serve the shrimp sizzling in the skillet.

EMPANADES
LAMB EMPANADAS WITH MOJO

In Catalonia, *empanades* are served everywhere, hot from the fryer, sometimes with dipping sauce and sometimes without. The most popular ones are from Galicia and stuffed with canned tuna, peppers, onions, and olives. One day, I had some leftover cuts and used lamb instead of tuna to make empanades. Everyone loved them, especially with the *mojo canaira*, a simple herb sauce from the Canary Islands made with fresh mint.

MOJO SAUCE

½ cup fresh mint leaves

¼ cup fresh cilantro leaves

¼ cup fresh curly parsley leaves

1½ teaspoons red wine vinegar

½ cup extra-virgin olive oil

Kosher salt and freshly ground black pepper

EMPANADES

2 tablespoons vegetable oil, plus about 6 cups for deep-frying

1 small yellow onion, finely chopped

½ russet potato (about 6 ounces), peeled and finely chopped

½ pound ground lamb

¼ cup pimiento-stuffed green olives, finely chopped

¼ cup finely chopped fresh cilantro

¼ cup finely chopped fresh curly parsley

1 small carrot (about 2 ounces), finely chopped

¾ cup Sofregit (page 34) or store-bought sofrito

1 teaspoon pimentón (smoked paprika)

1 teaspoon ground cumin

Kosher salt

About half of a 10-ounce package of 4-inch round wonton wrappers

1   Make the mojo sauce: In a blender or food processor, process the mint, cilantro, parsley, vinegar, and olive oil until smooth. Taste and season with salt and pepper until it tastes good to you.

2   For the empanades: In a large skillet, heat 2 tablespoons vegetable oil over medium-low heat. When the oil is shimmering, add the onion and cook until soft and translucent, 10 to 15 minutes, stirring occasionally. Add the potato and cook over medium heat until soft but still firm, 10 to 15 minutes, stirring often.

3   When the onion and potato are soft, stir the lamb into the pan and cook over medium heat until browned, about 6 minutes, breaking up the lamb with a spoon. Stir in the olives, cilantro, parsley, carrot, and sofregit and cook until the carrot is tender, about 8 minutes. Stir in the pimentón and cumin, then taste the mixture, adding salt until it tastes good to you. Cook until the mixture holds together when scooped with a serving spoon like a thick pasta sauce, maybe 2 minutes more. Remove from the heat and let cool.

4   To assemble the empanades, place one wonton wrapper on a work surface and fill it with 1 to 2 tablespoons of filling. Dip your fingertip in water, then run it along the outer edge of the wonton to moisten it. Fold the wonton over the filling to make a half-moon and pinch it closed to seal in the filling. Repeat with the remaining filling and wonton wrappers.

5   Heat 2 inches of vegetable oil in a large, heavy-bottomed pan over medium heat to 350°F. Adjust the heat as necessary to maintain the 350°F frying temperature. Working in batches, gently drop in the empanades and fry until crisp and golden brown all over, 3 to 5 minutes, turning with tongs.

6   Serve the empanades with a small bowl of mojo alongside for dipping.

EL CONSELL: After filling and sealing, you can fry the empanades right away, or cover and chill them for a few hours before frying, or freeze them for later. To freeze, arrange the empanades on a large sheet pan lined with parchment paper. Freeze until solid, about 1 hour, then transfer to a resealable bag. Frozen empanades can be fried directly from the freezer without thawing. Use within 3 months.

LES MILLORS LLAUNES

THE BEST OF TINS

If the only preserved fish you've ever eaten is canned tuna, it's time to branch out. The quality of Spanish seafood is second to none, and we capture it in our *conserves*, or tins. You might be surprised to find that seafood preserves very well. In Spain, fresh fish are immediately trimmed, cleaned, and sealed in small tins. We only pack the freshest seasonal seafood. If no fish comes to market, nothing gets preserved.

Catalans have a long history of canning the freshest local seafood and seasonal vegetables. You never know what will be available at any given time of year, and canning the best foods ensures you will be able to access them anytime you want to experience them again.

It may sound strange, but even the very best restaurants in Barcelona proudly display their *conserves*. I have so much respect for good-quality canned food that I named my tapas bar in Austin, Texas, Barlata—*lata* means "can" in Spanish. In Catalonia, we simply open up cans of the good stuff, but at Barlata, I play on that idea. I cook seafood dishes like octopus with potatoes, or squid stuffed with sausage, and serve them in attractive shallow tins. It's a fun way to honor my Catalan heritage and bring the tradition of quality tinned food to a broader audience.

Tinned seafood in Spain varies from region to region. The Catalan town of L'Escala is renowned for its fine anchovies, which locals have been preserving since before the Romans showed up. Further north in Cantabria, the anchovies are also quite good. They are usually harvested in April when the fish reaches peak flavor. Further west in Galicia, the sea brings some of the best clams and *escopinyes* (cockles) you'll find anywhere on the planet. The larger the cockles, the larger the can, and the more expensive they become. This seafood can get so pricey that shop owners keep their *escopinyes* locked in a cabinet behind the register. Just imagine that—canned food so high in value that it is kept under lock and key. It's that good!

The best tinned seafood is often served on weekends during *l'hora del vermut* or "vermouth hour" (see page 72). It's simply more convenient on a lazy Saturday or Sunday to open a tin from your pantry than to cook from scratch. To accompany chilled vermut, I love a mixed seafood plate of rich sardines packed in vinegar, *escopinyes*, tinned razor clams, mussels in olive oil, olives stuffed with anchovies, and seitons (Pickled Anchovies, page 47). Potato chips also bring great crunch. When you serve a few different *conserves* and snacks like this on a single plate, it's called *popurri*. It tastes fantastic drizzled with a tangy sauce of 1 teaspoon pimentón (smoked paprika) mixed with 1 tablespoon extra-virgin olive oil, 2 tablespoons red wine vinegar, and maybe a few drops of hot sauce. If you are in Barcelona craving delicious seafood, stop in a restaurant during *l'hora del vermut* and order the popurri.

Of course, brands like the jolly Green Giant don't sell these kinds of canned foods. The best *conserves* are found in small Hispanic markets that import high-quality tins from Spain. My friend Pere Selles has a terrific line of tinned seafood called Matiz that I highly recommend. Or, if you're traveling in Catalonia, seek out the best tins in old-fashioned *botiga de queviures*. These small, family-owned shops specialize in traditional Catalan foods and tend to be the best source for tinned seafood, pickled vegetables, and other good-quality *conserves*.

CALAMARS FREGITS
FRIED SQUID WITH FENNEL

In Spain, we have a tradition of deep-frying fish called *pescadito frito*. In Catalan, we say *fregits* instead of *frito* (which is the Spanish term). Every tapas bar in Catalonia serves *calamars fregits*, and in this version, I add some sliced fresh fennel for extra crunch and a hint of its enchanting anise aroma. The fennel gets fried and served with the squid, adding to the flavor and texture of the dish. If you want to serve it to a crowd, the recipe doubles easily.

2 cups all-purpose flour

1 tablespoon paprika

1½ teaspoons garlic powder

1½ teaspoons onion powder

¾ teaspoon cayenne pepper

¼ small fennel bulb, cored and thinly sliced lengthwise (about ¼ cup)

1 cup buttermilk

¼ cup Allioli (page 32) or store-bought aioli

Finely grated zest of 1 lime

About 6 cups vegetable oil, for deep-frying

½ cup squid bodies, sliced into rings and tentacles (about 4 ounces)

Kosher or flaky sea salt, for serving

1 In a large bowl, whisk together the flour, paprika, garlic powder, onion powder, and cayenne. In a small bowl, combine the fennel and buttermilk. In a small serving bowl, combine the allioli and lime zest.

2 Heat 2 inches of oil in a large heavy-bottomed pan over medium heat to 350°F. Adjust the heat as necessary to maintain the 350°F frying temperature. Use a slotted spoon to scoop up about half the fennel pieces, allowing the excess liquid to drip off. Transfer to the flour mixture, tossing gently, shaking the bowl, and using your fingers to evenly coat the pieces and keep them separated. Transfer the coated pieces to a mesh strainer, such as a spider strainer for frying. Repeat with half of the squid, tossing it in the flour mixture and transferring it to the strainer. Tap and shake the strainer gently, jostling the coated squid and fennel, allowing excess flour to fall away.

3 Use the strainer to gently lower the floured squid and fennel into the hot oil, tipping to release them. Fry just long enough to cook the fish and turn the breading golden brown, about 1 minute. Repeat with the remaining squid and fennel, transferring the cooked pieces to paper towels to drain as they are done.

4 Sprinkle with salt. Serve warm with the lime allioli alongside for dipping.

PINXO MORÚ

LAMB BROCHETTES

Pinxos are skewered foods usually displayed in Catalan bars, buffet-style, for guests to nibble on while drinking. Traditionally, the bartender keeps track of how much to charge you by how many skewers you leave on the bar. *Pinxo morú* are a bit larger than other pinxos, similar to a kebab. These feature the Moroccan flavors of paprika, cumin, and garlic, a sort of Catalan tip of the hat to the deep influence of the Moors in Catalonia. The only departure from the traditional dish here is that I top my cucumber-yogurt salad and pinxos with spicy pepper sauce. What can I say? I like it hot.

MARINATED LAMB

1 tablespoon finely chopped fresh cilantro

2 teaspoons paprika

2 teaspoons kosher salt

1 teaspoon ground cumin

1 garlic clove, chopped

1 tablespoon fresh lime juice

3 tablespoons extra-virgin olive oil

1 pound boneless leg of lamb or top round, cut into 1-inch cubes

PEPPER SAUCE

2 dried árbol chiles

1 roasted red bell pepper

1 cup Sofregit (page 34) or store-bought sofrito

¼ cup extra-virgin olive oil

1 tablespoon fresh lime juice

1 teaspoon ground cumin

Kosher salt

CUCUMBER-YOGURT SALAD

¼ cup plain whole-milk yogurt

1 tablespoon chopped fresh mint leaves

Kosher salt

½ medium English cucumber, peeled, seeded, and thinly sliced on the diagonal

8 to 10 skewers (6- to 8-inch), soaked in water for 1 hour if wooden

1 Marinate the lamb: In a large resealable bag, combine the cilantro, paprika, salt, cumin, garlic, lime juice, and olive oil. Add the lamb and shake to coat. Press the air out of the bag and seal. Marinate in the refrigerator for at least 4 hours or overnight.

2 Make the pepper sauce: Bring a small saucepan of water to a boil over high heat. Add the chiles, remove the pan from the heat, and let stand until the chiles are soft, about 20 minutes.

3 Pluck the chiles from the water and transfer to a blender or food processor. Add the roasted red pepper, sofregit, olive oil, lime juice, and cumin. Season generously with salt and pulse until the mixture is thick and smooth. It should be thick enough to rest on the plate in a thick pool.

4 Meanwhile, make the cucumber-yogurt salad: In a medium bowl, stir together the yogurt, mint, and a generous pinch of salt. Add the cucumber and toss to coat. Use immediately or chill for up to 3 hours.

5 Heat a grill or grill pan to medium. Thread 4 to 5 pieces of marinated lamb onto each skewer. Grill the skewers until the meat is charred in spots but still rare inside, about 10 minutes, turning once.

6 Divide the dressed cucumbers among plates and top with the skewers. Spoon on the pepper sauce.

L'HORA DEL VERMUT

VERMOUTH HOUR

Table wines only last a few days once you open them. But adding spirits raises the alcohol content, making the wine more shelf-stable so it lasts longer. When you "fortify" wine in this way with spirits, sugar, and a handful of herbs, roots, and aromatics, it transforms the drink into vermouth, or as we say in Catalan, *vermut*.

Bottles of house-made vermouth are poured in bodegas all over Catalonia, set on tables under umbrellas, and gulped as refreshment after trips *a la platja* (to the beach). But nowhere is this chilled drink more revered than during *l'hora del vermut* (vermouth hour). This time in Catalonia is traditionally reserved for Saturdays and Sundays, often after going to church and before having lunch. That's right: First we confess, then we go drinking. *L'hora del vermut* is the time for family and friends to unwind and share news of the week over a drink.

Of course, it's always nice to have a few nibbles as well. To complement the mildly sweet, herbal taste of the vermouth, the best snacks bring sharp, salty flavors. Pickled vegetables, potato chips, olives, and various types of tinned seafood make the perfect accompaniments during *l'hora del vermut*. These foods open your appetite for the bigger meal to follow. Over the past few decades, this tradition had largely been forgotten in Barcelona, but it is now hip again. Meeting friends for "vermouth hour" has become trendy, and chefs have even created special bars to revitalize this old Catalan custom.

Perhaps you would like to try it at home? All you need are friends, snacks, and homemade vermouth. In Catalonia, vermouth begins with white wine, though the color of the wine will darken a bit after the fortifying process. Whether your vermouth ends up tasting sweet or dry depends on the residual sugar in the base wine and how much caramelized sugar you add to balance the bitterness of the spices you use. Either way, the secret to great homemade vermut is your signature brew of spices. The mix can vary, including everything from clove, coriander, and cardamom to orange peel, bay leaves, and juniper berries. Experiment with your favorites, but do not skip gentian root and wormwood. These spices give vermut its unique bitterness and flavor, and they are easily obtained online. For snacks to serve during *l'hora del vermut*, focus on bright, salty flavors, including at least a few types of high-quality tinned seafood such as those described in "The Best of Tins" on page 65.

VERMUT DE LA CASA

HOMEMADE SWEET VERMOUTH

MAKES ABOUT 1 QUART

¼ cup sugar

1 bottle (750 ml) dry white wine, such as Pinot Grigio

Zest of 1 orange, peeled in strips with a vegetable peeler

1 sprig of fresh rosemary

5 black peppercorns

2 whole star anise

2 whole cloves

1 cinnamon stick

1 bay leaf

½ teaspoon wormwood leaf

½ teaspoon roughly chopped gentian root

¼ teaspoon coriander seeds

½ cup brandy

½ cup cream sherry, such as sweetened Oloroso

1 Line a sheet pan with parchment paper or a silicone baking mat.

2 In a small saucepan, stir together the sugar and 2 tablespoons water over medium-low heat until the sugar dissolves, 3 to 4 minutes. Increase the heat to medium and simmer until the liquid turns medium-dark amber in color, about 4 minutes, swirling the pan occasionally. Stand back and pour in ¼ cup of the wine (it will sizzle and foam wildly). When it settles down, stir until it is incorporated into the caramel. Pour the caramel onto the lined baking sheet and let stand until it is cool to the touch, about 30 minutes. Break or crush the caramel into small shards.

3 In a small saucepan, combine 1 cup of the wine with the orange zest, rosemary, peppercorns, star anise, whole cloves, cinnamon stick, bay leaf, wormwood, gentian, and coriander seeds. Bring to a boil over medium-high heat, then remove the pan from the heat and stir in the caramel pieces. Cover and let steep at room temperature for at least 1 hour or overnight, stirring occasionally.

4 Strain the herb-infused wine through a fine-mesh sieve into a pitcher or large bowl, discarding the solids. Stir in the remaining wine along with the brandy and sherry.

5 Pour the vermut back into the wine bottle and replace the cork. The vermut won't all fit, so drink whatever is left. *Salut!* Store the bottle of vermut in the refrigerator for up to 1 month.

BIQUINI MALLORQUÍ

GRILLED MANCHEGO AND SAUSAGE SANDWICH

SERVES 2 TO 4
(MAKES 1 SANDWICH)

This sandwich was originally named for the Bikini concert hall in Barcelona's Les Corts district. The hall opened in 1953 as a place for dancing and dining, and became known for its adaptation of the French croque-monsieur sandwich. You can still enjoy *biquini* sandwiches in tapas bars around Barcelona and throughout Catalonia. This version celebrates *sobrassada*, a cured sausage from the Spanish island of Mallorca with a soft, spreadable texture similar to Italy's 'nduja. For a more traditional biquini, use a few thin slices of Serrano ham instead.

2 thin slices peasant bread or Farmer's Bread (page 236)

2 teaspoons Dijon mustard

2 ounces Manchego cheese, thinly sliced

2 ounces sobrassada or 'nduja

2 tablespoons salted butter, at room temperature

Olives, such as Arbequina, for serving (optional)

1   Spread one side of one slice of bread with the mustard and top with the cheese. Spread the sobrassada on the other slice of bread. Sandwich the bread slices together and coat the exterior of the sandwich with butter.

2   Heat a medium cast-iron skillet over medium heat. Add the sandwich and cook until it is golden brown on the bottom, about 4 minutes, shaking the pan once or twice for more even browning. Flip the sandwich and repeat on the other side, about 4 minutes more, reducing the heat to medium-low if the bread threatens to burn. Transfer the sandwich to a cutting board and cut it into 4 pieces. Serve warm with olives, if desired.

XATÓ

PENEDÈS SALAD

This salad is a specialty from the Penedès and Garraf regions, and the pride of my hometown. Several towns comprise la Ruta del Xató—including Vilafranca del Penedès, Vilanova i la Geltrú, Sitges, El Vendrell, and Calafell—and every winter, the towns along the route compete to see who makes the best salad. The competition is a big event celebrating our food traditions and it occurs along with music festivals, wine tours, and other special events. The ingredients and presentation vary among towns and cooks, but the salad always contains shredded salt cod, tuna, and frisée, and it is often served either on top of or alongside a small omelet, like Catalan Potato and Onion Omelet (page 55). Of course, I think our Penedès version of the salad is the best.

½ cup Romesco (page 32) or store-bought romesco sauce

1 tablespoon sherry vinegar

3 tablespoons extra-virgin olive oil

1 to 2 large heads (½ pound) frisée lettuce, trimmed and torn into bite-size pieces

4 ounces salt cod, desalted (see page 157), drained, and shredded into bite-size pieces

1 can (6 ounces) bonito tuna in olive oil, drained and flaked into large pieces

8 oil-packed anchovy fillets

20 black olives (about 1 cup), halved lengthwise and pitted

1 Place the romesco in a large bowl and slowly whisk in the vinegar and oil in a thin, steady stream until the mixture thickens slightly. Add the frisée pieces, shredded salt cod, and tuna and use your hands to gently toss the salad until it is evenly coated in dressing.

2 To serve, pick up a portion of salad with your hands and shake it to remove any excess dressing; divide the portions among four plates. Top the salads with anchovies and olives and spoon any remaining dressing from the salad bowl over the top.

EL CONSELL: For the canned bonito tuna in olive oil, I like the Matiz brand, one of my favorite imports. Their anchovies are pretty good too.

ENSALADILLA RUSSA

RUSSIAN TUNA SALAD

This tuna salad is usually served at the center of the table with crackers and bite-size crispy breadsticks called *picos* for dipping. As you nibble, you trade bites of salad with sips of cava. You could also spoon the salad onto toasted peasant bread for a fantastic sandwich. This recipe was loaned to me by my chef friend Jordi Vila, whose version pairs perfectly with a cold beer from the Moritz brewery in Barcelona.

1 small russet potato (about 4 ounces), unpeeled

Kosher salt

6 ounces thin green beans or haricots verts, trimmed and cut into ½-inch pieces

1 medium carrot, peeled and finely diced

4 large eggs

About ⅔ cup mayonnaise

1 can (6 ounces) bonito tuna in olive oil, drained and flaked into large pieces

Freshly ground black pepper

2 tablespoons finely sliced fresh chives

A pinch of pimentón (smoked paprika)

1   Prepare a large bowl with ice water. In a medium saucepan, combine the whole potato with cold water to cover, and season the water generously with salt. Bring to a boil over medium-high heat and cook until the potato is tender, about 15 minutes. Reserving the water in the saucepan, use a slotted spoon or spider strainer to transfer the potato to the ice water until it is cool enough to handle, about 10 minutes.

2   Reserving the ice bath, dry the potato with a paper towel. Peel and dice the potato into ¾-inch cubes and place in a medium bowl.

3   Return the water in the saucepan to a boil, add the beans and carrot, and cook until the carrot is crisp-tender and brightly colored, 3 to 4 minutes. Drain the vegetables and transfer them to the ice bath to cool.

4   Place the eggs in the same saucepan and cover with cold water. Place the saucepan over medium heat and cook just until the water begins to boil with one big bubble. Remove the saucepan from the heat, cover, and let stand for 12 minutes. Remove the eggs from the hot water and run under cold water until the eggs are cool enough to handle. Peel the eggs and finely chop 3 of them.

5   Add the chopped eggs, mayonnaise, and tuna to the bowl with the potato. Drain the carrots and green beans, pat dry, and add to the bowl. Season generously with salt and pepper and stir to combine. Taste the salad and add more mayonnaise as needed (the salad should be very creamy and soft).

6   Before serving, coarsely grate the remaining egg on top of the salad. Garnish with sliced chives and a pinch of pimentón.

TIRADITO AMB ESCALIVADA

SPANISH SASHIMI WITH ROASTED VEGETABLE PUREES

SERVES 4 TO 6
AS A FIRST COURSE

I love sushi, as do many Spaniards. Japanese flavors make sense to me because you can taste the love of the sea and the love of rice in every bite. This is my Spanish take on Japanese sashimi: thin slices of raw fish served with roasted vegetable purees and a shower of crunchy *cancha* (toasted Peruvian corn). For the fish, I like to use escolar because it is mild and fatty like tuna and slices easily, though sushi-grade ahi tuna or yellowtail could be substituted. If you have trouble finding the cancha, you could use corn nuts instead.

1 medium red bell pepper
1 medium yellow bell pepper
1 small globe eggplant (about 10 ounces)
About ½ cup extra-virgin olive oil
Kosher salt
1 pound sushi-grade escolar, ahi tuna, or yellowtail fillet
½ lemon
¼ cup cancha or corn nuts, chopped
Garlic Oil (page 28) or extra-virgin olive oil, for serving
Fresh curly parsley leaves, for garnish
Flaky sea salt, such as Maldon, for serving

1   Heat the broiler with a rack in the highest position in the oven.

2   Place the bell peppers on a sheet pan and broil until softened and blackened all over, about 15 minutes, turning a few times. Transfer the peppers to a heatproof bowl and cover with plastic wrap. Let the peppers stand until wilted and cool enough to handle, about 5 minutes. Leave the oven on for the eggplant, but reduce the oven temperature to 350°F.

3   Place the eggplant on a sheet pan and bake it until it is very soft, about 40 minutes. Transfer the baked eggplant to a cutting board and let cool, about 20 minutes.

4   Meanwhile, remove the skin, seeds, and membranes from the cooled peppers. Transfer the peeled red pepper to a blender or food processor and add 2 tablespoons of the olive oil and ½ teaspoon salt. Pulse until the mixture is slightly chunky. Repeat with the yellow pepper and another 2 tablespoons olive oil to make two separate purees.

5   Chill four to six small plates.

6   Cut the eggplant in half, then use a spoon to scoop out the flesh and transfer it to a blender or food processor. Add another 2 tablespoons olive oil and 1 teaspoon salt. Blend until the mixture is relatively smooth with the consistency of a thick puree, adding more olive oil if necessary so that the mixture is creamy but holds its shape on a spoon.

7   Carefully cut the fish into even slices ⅛ inch thick. Arrange the fish slices on the chilled plates and squeeze a few drops of lemon juice over each serving. Spoon some of each puree around the fish and top with the chopped cancha. Garnish with the garlic oil, parsley, and flaky salt.

CARN CRUA

BARLATA CARPACCIO

SERVES 4 TO 6
AS A FIRST COURSE

The success of this dish—a carpaccio-style beef with Spanish flair—depends on the quality and fattiness of the beef you use. I like to use Wagyu. Instead of the pricey tenderloin, sometimes I use shoulder tender roast, which is often called a teres major cut. Either way, trim the meat of all excess fat so you're left with only pure beef. Quickly seared with a torch or on a hot *planxa*, the beef takes on more flavor while still maintaining its tenderness. This recipe has several components—fried garlic chips, pickled mushrooms, crunchy onions, a sherry-soy sauce, and the beef itself—but the dish is well worth the effort for a special occasion. Start it a few days ahead of time so the mushrooms can fully pickle.

PICKLED MUSHROOMS

1 cup cava vinegar or champagne vinegar

½ cup apple cider vinegar

1½ teaspoons coriander seeds

1½ teaspoons mustard seeds

1 teaspoon Dijon mustard

¼ cup honey

2 sprigs fresh thyme

Kosher salt

1 cup sliced shiitake mushrooms (about 3 ounces)

BEEF

1 piece (12 ounces) Wagyu beef tenderloin or teres major, trimmed

Kosher salt

SHERRY SAUCE

1 cup Fino sherry

2 teaspoons soy sauce

2 teaspoons mirin

½ teaspoon rice vinegar

1 teaspoon fresh lemon juice

GARLIC CHIPS

¾ cup vegetable oil

¼ cup extra-virgin olive oil

6 to 8 garlic cloves, peeled and very thinly sliced

Kosher salt

Flaky sea salt, such as Maldon, for serving

¼ small yellow onion, thinly sliced

1   Pickle the mushrooms: In a medium saucepan, combine the cava vinegar, cider vinegar, coriander, mustard seeds, Dijon mustard, honey, thyme, and 2 tablespoons salt. Bring to a boil over high heat, stirring to mix everything together. Place the mushrooms in a heatproof medium bowl and pour the hot pickling liquid over them. Cool slightly, then cover the bowl with plastic wrap and refrigerate for at least 3 days or up to 2 weeks before using. The mushrooms will become smaller, dense slices.

PICA-PICA

82

2 Prepare the beef: About 2 hours before serving, prepare a medium bowl of ice water. Generously season the beef all over with salt and let stand 5 minutes. Use a blowtorch to quickly sear the surface of the beef until it is just barely browned. (Alternatively, heat a cast-iron skillet over high heat until it is screaming hot and dab the beef on all its surfaces, rotating almost constantly and working very quickly, until the meat is lightly browned all over but still raw inside.) Plunge the meat into the ice water to stop the cooking and let stand until chilled, about 1 minute. Remove the meat and pat it dry. Wrap the meat in plastic and place it in the refrigerator until firm, about 1 hour.

3 Make the sherry sauce: In a small saucepan, combine the sherry, soy sauce, and mirin. Bring to a simmer over medium-low heat and cook until the alcohol burns off, 5 to 7 minutes. Remove the pan from the heat and stir in the rice vinegar and lemon juice.

4 Make the garlic chips: In a small saucepan, heat the oils over medium heat. When the oil is shimmering, add the garlic, stirring constantly to be sure the garlic swims freely in the oil. Reduce the heat to low and cook until the garlic chips are evenly golden brown and they sizzle less aggressively, 6 to 8 minutes. Strain the chips through a small colander, reserving the garlic-flavored oil in a glass mason jar (it will keep for several weeks in the refrigerator). Turn the garlic chips out onto a paper towel to drain, and season with salt.

5 Chill four to six small plates.

6 Using a sharp, thin knife, slice the beef as carefully and thinly as you can while keeping each slice in a whole piece. Working with one piece at a time, place a beef slice flat on a work surface and gently flatten the meat by pressing the flat side of the knife into it. The meat should become so thin it is transparent in spots.

7 Carefully arrange and overlap the slices, about 8 per serving, on the chilled plates. Sprinkle the meat with sea salt, spoon the sherry sauce over the top, and scatter over a few pickled mushrooms and garlic chips. Dip the onion in the mushroom-pickling liquid for about 1 minute, then scatter the slices over the beef. Drizzle each plate lightly with some of the garlic oil from the garlic chips and serve.

VERDURES I LLEGUMS
VEGETABLES AND BEANS

The freshness and quality of our local produce is a point of pride in Catalonia. For example, we don't import tomatoes from other countries—we wait until they are ready to enjoy from our own bushes and vines. From the community fire to the salad bowl, vegetables and beans play important roles in Catalan meals. Vegetables are incorporated into most main dishes but also form the very foundation of traditional Catalan foods, such as those served at the annual *calçotada* (page 92), a springtime celebration of the region's unique green onions, or *calçots*, which are roasted in hot, smoky embers and then dipped in *romesco* (page 32).

GASPATXO
GAZPACHO

Some cooks will tell you to let gaspatxo sit for an extended period of time, but I think it is best served within a few hours. I like the flavors to stay clean and somewhat separate—without all the ingredients melding together into one taste. It is very important to build the flavors as you go so you don't end up with a runny salsa or a simple tomato puree. If you're making gaspatxo in the summer, by all means use ripe heirloom tomatoes. The rest of the year, use canned tomatoes for the best taste.

2 slices baguette bread, crusts removed

1 cup almonds, toasted

4 garlic cloves

½ cup fresh mint leaves

1 English cucumber, peeled, seeded, and cut into 1-inch pieces

1 medium red onion, cut into 1-inch pieces

1 medium red bell pepper, cut into 1-inch pieces

1 medium yellow bell pepper, cut into 1-inch pieces

1 medium green bell pepper, cut into 1-inch pieces

10 red vine or heirloom tomatoes, cored, or 1 (28-ounce) can whole peeled tomatoes in juice

½ cup extra-virgin olive oil, plus more for finishing

1 to 3 tablespoons red wine vinegar, to taste

Kosher salt and freshly ground black pepper

1   Place the bread in a medium bowl and add enough cold water to soak the slices (about ½ cup). Let sit until softened, about 5 minutes.

2   In a food processor, combine the almonds, garlic, and mint and pulse until the mixture resembles wet sand, about 2 minutes. Squeeze the water from the soaked bread until it no longer drips, then add the bread to the processor and blend until very smooth and creamy, another minute or two. Add the cucumber, onion, and bell peppers and pulse until the vegetables are finely chopped but not pureed. Transfer the mixture to a large bowl.

3   Add the tomatoes (plus the juice if using canned), olive oil, and vinegar to the food processor and pulse until finely chopped. Stir the tomato mixture into the bowl of chopped vegetables and season with salt and pepper. Taste and season with more vinegar or oil if needed.

4   Cover the bowl with plastic wrap and refrigerate until chilled, at least 2 hours or up to 8 hours. Before serving, taste the soup and adjust the seasoning with more vinegar, salt, and pepper. Serve in small bowls, drizzled with a little more olive oil to finish.

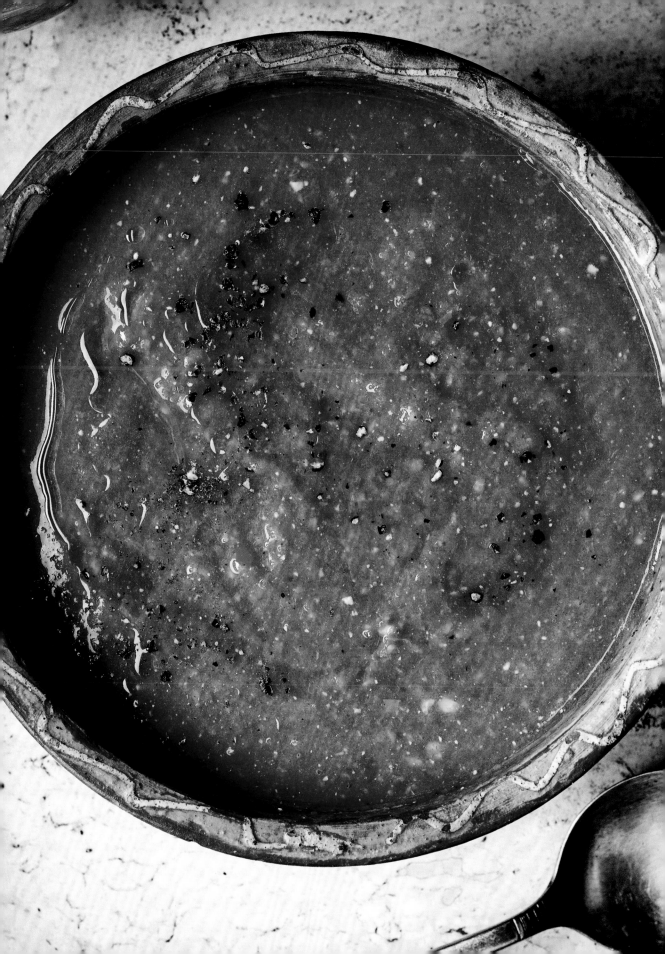

KALE A LA CATALANA

BRAISED KALE WITH PINE NUTS AND CURRANTS

Catalans love to add dried fruit and nuts to humble dishes to make them worthy of the holiday table, a practice often employed with roasted birds, such as Roasted Chicken in a Dutch Oven (page 176). This recipe also shares that tradition with vegetarians: Serve it with Stewed Chickpeas with Spinach (page 101) to make a vegetarian meal. I love kale in this dish because it holds its texture well even when braised, but you could also use spinach, which is more traditionally Catalan.

1 tablespoon extra-virgin olive oil, plus more for serving

1 tablespoon vegetable oil

3 to 4 bunches lacinato kale or curly kale, stemmed and torn into 2-inch pieces

2 tablespoons pine nuts, toasted

¼ cup dried currants

2 garlic cloves, finely chopped

½ cup Vegetable Stock (page 35) or store-bought vegetable stock

Kosher salt and freshly ground black pepper

1   In a large skillet, heat the oils over medium-high heat. When the oil is shimmering, add the kale and cook until it begins to wilt and brown in spots, about 5 minutes, stirring occasionally.

2   Stir in the pine nuts, currants, garlic, and stock. Bring to a simmer and cook until the kale is tender and the stock has almost completely evaporated, about 5 minutes, tossing once or twice. Season with salt and pepper and drizzle with a little more olive oil before serving.

BOLETS A LA LLAUNA

ROASTED MUSHROOMS WITH GARLIC AND PARSLEY

Like "paella," the term *llauna* refers to both the dish and the pan used to make it. The traditional llauna pan is a piece of thin sheet metal with the edges turned up. Here we use a more common sheet pan. Be sure to keep the mushrooms in a single layer so each one makes contact with the pan and browns, developing deep flavor. The parsley here is also roasted, a typical Catalan technique for when herbs are served with chunks of salt cod or snails. I like to serve this dish with chunks of bread, such as *pa de pagès* (Farmer's Bread, page 236).

6 to 8 garlic cloves, roughly chopped

1 teaspoon kosher salt

Leaves from 1 bunch fresh curly parsley (about 3 cups)

6 tablespoons extra-virgin olive oil, plus more for drizzling

12 ounces mixed chanterelle, oyster, and/or shiitake mushrooms, stems trimmed

1   Preheat the oven to 500°F.

2   Make a *picada* by mashing the garlic and salt to a fine paste in a mortar with a pestle. Gradually add in the parsley leaves, mashing each addition completely before adding more, until you have a green paste. Stir in the olive oil. Scrape the picada onto a large sheet pan. Add the mushrooms, toss until thoroughly coated, and arrange the mushrooms in a single layer.

3   Roast until the mushrooms are browned and have shrunk to about half their size, 8 to 10 minutes, shaking the pan once or twice for even browning.

4   It is traditional to serve this dish right on the llauna or sheet pan as you would do with a dish cooked in a cast-iron skillet. The sheet pan helps to retain all of the olive oil and mushroom juices.

AMANIDA A LA GRAELLA
GRILLED SALAD

SERVES 4
AS A SIDE DISH

My friend chef Jordi Vila recently took me to his brother-in-law's farm and cooked a dinner I will never forget. He set up a fire in one of the orchards and made a grilled escarole salad with vinaigrette from grilled lemons. It was a modern take on the *escalivada* we had when I was a kid (see page 92), with the same feeling of strong community and good food. Jordi insists I share his secret: The difference between a good escalivada and a bad one is that the grilled vegetables can touch neither water nor the vinaigrette until just before serving.

½ navel orange

½ lemon

1 large head escarole (about 12 ounces), halved lengthwise
with stem end intact

4 fresh figs, halved lengthwise

2 garlic cloves, peeled

Kosher salt and freshly ground black pepper

6 tablespoons extra-virgin olive oil

1   Heat a grill or grill pan to medium (see note). Grill the orange and lemon until the peels char and begin to split, about 8 minutes, turning them occasionally. Remove to a cutting board and let cool.

2   Meanwhile, grill the escarole, cut-side down, until it is charred in spots, about 30 seconds. Remove to a platter cut-side up and let cool. While the escarole cools, grill the figs cut-side down until they are charred in spots, about 30 seconds. Remove to the platter cut-side up and let cool.

3   Squeeze the juice from the lemon and orange into a medium bowl. Mash the garlic in a mortar with a pestle and scrape it into the bowl with the citrus juice. Add a few generous pinches of salt and pepper. Begin whisking, then slowly add a few drops of oil, whisking constantly. As the mixture thickens, add the oil a bit faster, still whisking constantly. Pour the vinaigrette over the salad and serve immediately.

EL CONSELL: If you can, grill the citrus and escarole over a wood fire in a fire pit. You can even char the fruit right near the embers of the fire. The flavor of the smoke will enhance the taste of the dish, and the experience of the fire will set your mind to dreaming.

ESCALIVADA I CALÇOTADA

VEGETABLES ROASTED IN THE EMBERS

Growing up in my neighborhood, on the outskirts of Vilafranca del Penedès, it was typical for the men to make an outdoor fire with trimmings from the vineyards nearby. They would pile the pruned vines in the middle of the dirt road at the end of the *barri* (neighborhood). The vines would catch fire quickly, then hush into glowing embers. The older men, a glass of wine in one hand and a stick for stoking the flames in the other, would tell the younger kids to run back and report to their mothers: The fire was ready. The neighborhood ladies would emerge from their homes with aprons full of vegetables—zucchini, peppers, eggplant, tomatoes, onions, and *calçots* (a spring onion unique to Catalonia)—ready to nestle the vegetables into the hot embers. The vegetables would blacken on their surfaces and gradually soften inside as the conversation sparked along. These ember-roasted vegetables would be used in meals over the next several days—pounded into sauces, stirred into *paelles,* or even just drizzled with olive oil and sprinkled with flaky sea salt. It was cooking with a side of community.

Once a year, this neighborhood roast grew into a giant feast called a *calçotada*, a barbecue held for the express purpose of celebrating Catalonia's most beloved vegetable. These unique green onions are available only during springtime in Catalonia, especially near the city of Tarragona, and excitement for calçots compares to the eagerness for springtime ramps in New England. Calçots have straight bulbs and resemble young leeks. They are planted in trenches and buried with more and more soil as their shoots grow out of the ground. At a calçotada, the onions are grilled in the embers (or over them), then wrapped in newspaper and served on roofing tiles with romesco sauce. To eat them, you peel back the charred outer layers of the onion and dip the tender inner white parts in the creamy sauce. As with all Catalan festivities, cava sparkling wine is always served alongside.

To host your own calçotada, you could use Mexican green onions (spring onions), which are nearly the right thickness and have slightly bulbous ends. Plan on two bunches per person along with about ¼ cup Romesco (page 32) per person for dipping. It's best to roast the calçots right in the embers of a wood fire, or directly over the flames, so they absorb plenty of smoky aroma. In a pinch, you could just blacken the onions on a grill or in a grill pan. Either way, prepare a wood fire or preheat a grill or a grill pan for medium-high heat. Grill the onions directly over the heat until they are charred all over and tender inside, turning them now and then. It will take 8 to 10 minutes total. As they are done, wrap the onions in sheets of newspaper and let them cool in their own steam for a few minutes to soften them a bit more. Enjoy them directly from the paper by peeling back the outermost charred layers of onion and dipping the tender core in romesco sauce.

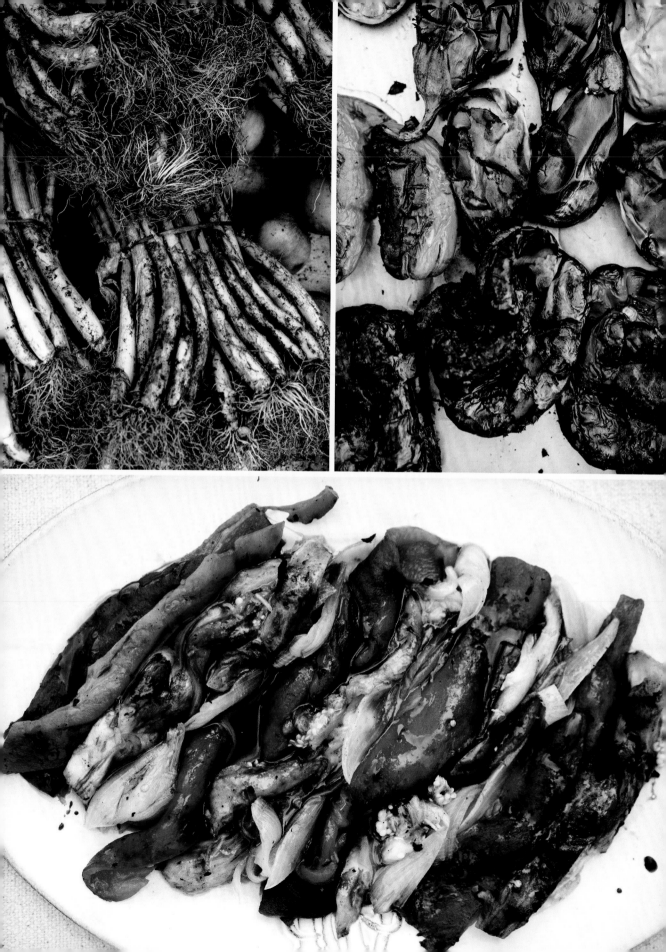

PATATES A LA SAL

WRINKLY POTATOES

These potatoes are cooked in very salty water—salty like the sea, according to grandmothers from the Canary Islands. By the time they are cooked through, the salt water evaporates, and the potato skins become wrinkled and covered with a white dusting of salt. Use fingerling or baby potatoes to be sure they become tender all the way through. If you like, make extra and keep them in the fridge to use for Monkfish and Potatoes in Browned Garlic Sauce (page 151) or Warm Octopus with Potatoes (page 146).

2½ pounds fingerling or small new potatoes
½ cup kosher salt
Allioli (page 32) or store-bought aioli, for serving

1   Place the potatoes in a deep, narrow saucepan or stockpot and add enough water to cover. Stir in the salt. Bring to a boil over high heat and cook, partially covered, until the water reduces to a thin layer below the potatoes, about 30 minutes. Uncover, reduce the heat to medium, and simmer until the water evaporates and the potatoes are very tender and coated in a white dusting of salt, about 30 minutes more. Remove the potatoes to a cutting board and let cool.

2   When the potatoes are cool enough to handle, wipe the excess salt from their surfaces using a dry kitchen towel. Cut the potatoes in half and serve with allioli for dipping, or let the potatoes cool to room temperature and store in an airtight container in the refrigerator for up to 2 days.

LA BOTÌGA DE LLEGUMS I L'AIGUA DE PLUJA

THE BEAN STORE AND CATALAN RAINWATER

When I return home now to the vibrant and diverse wine country of Penedès, it's hard to tell that, until the seventies or so, much of Catalan society was isolated. The towns outside Barcelona were very rural and the country's dictator, Francisco Franco, oppressed our culture, making economic development impossible. Decades of isolation caused Catalan food traditions—and the families who nurtured them—to be very humble and frugal. Meat was rarely brought home from the market. Instead, dried beans and lentils, *els llegums*, became a big part of the traditional Catalan diet—and still are to this day.

As kids, my siblings and I would be sent to the bean store once a week. The bean store sold only dried beans and had thirty to forty giant burlap sacks on the floor, each filled with buttery chickpeas, russet-colored favas, and various white beans such as *garrofó*, the kind traditionally used in Valencian Paella (page 114). Each sack had a big scoop in it and the beans were sold by weight on an antique scale.

When we got home with our bean bags, my mother would set aside some of the beans for later and the rest she would pour into a bowl of rainwater to soak. Many of the women on our street collected rainwater in barrels so that the flavor of their beans would be pure. Tap water was not for drinking or cooking—we didn't have mineral water, and the natural springs were too far from home. To prepare our daily beans, the core protein in our modest diet, the only water deemed trustworthy enough came from the heavens above. Today, of course, there is better water available in Catalonia. Many housewives use bottled water, or they just open the tap if the water coming from their faucets tastes good enough for their beans.

FAVES AMB PÈSOLS

FRESH FAVAS WITH PEAS

SERVES 6
AS A SIDE DISH
OR 4 AS A MAIN DISH

The classic version of this dish includes sautéed *morcilla* sausage, but sometimes I skip the sausage to make it vegetarian. If you do want to include it (which would make Catalans very proud), add it along with the onions and use pork stock instead of vegetable stock. And if you can't find fresh favas, frozen baby limas can be substituted. The liquor is optional, but it adds some dimension to this otherwise very bright dish. My mother always liked to sneak a dash of brandy into her cooking, so these flavors remind me of her.

2 tablespoons extra-virgin olive oil, plus more for drizzling

1 bunch spring onions (about 5), bulbs only, halved lengthwise

1 cup shelled and peeled fresh fava beans

1 cup shelled fresh green peas or thawed frozen peas

1½ cups Vegetable Stock (page 35) or store-bought vegetable stock

1 teaspoon finely sliced fresh mint

Dash of grappa or brandy (optional)

Flaky sea salt, for serving

1   In a medium saucepan, heat the oil over medium-high heat. When the oil is shimmering, add the onions and cook until they begin to soften, about 3 minutes, stirring often. Stir in the favas, peas, and stock. Increase the heat to high and bring to a boil. Cook until the favas and peas are tender and only a few spoonfuls of stock remain in the pan, about 8 minutes. Stir in the mint and grappa (if using).

2   Divide the beans among bowls and top each serving with some olive oil and flaky salt.

SAMFAINA

CATALAN VEGETABLE RAGOUT

Samfaina is the Catalan equivalent of southern French ratatouille. It is often paired with simple dishes such as Salt Cod Fritters with Pear Aioli (page 161) or Griddled Secreto Ibérico (page 226). It can even be served as a dip alongside Pureed Salt Cod with Mashed Potatoes (page 154). Be sure to add the pimentón after the dish is finished simmering—it prevents the spice from developing a bitter taste.

1 medium globe eggplant (about 1 pound), peeled and cut into ½-inch cubes

Kosher salt

1 cup extra-virgin olive oil

2 medium yellow onions, halved and thinly sliced

4 large garlic cloves, finely chopped

1 red bell pepper, cut into ½-inch pieces

1 green bell pepper, cut into ½-inch pieces

1 medium zucchini, cut into 1-inch pieces

1 can (14.5 ounces) chopped tomatoes, drained

1 teaspoon pimentón (smoked paprika)

1   Line a sheet pan with a few layers of paper towels. Arrange the eggplant in a single layer on the paper towels and sprinkle generously with salt. Set aside until the eggplant appears to sweat, releasing its liquid, about 30 minutes. Pat the eggplant dry with a clean paper towel.

2   In a large Dutch oven, heat ½ cup of the oil over medium heat. When the oil is shimmering, add the onions, season them with salt, and reduce the heat to low. Cook the onions slowly until they are translucent, about 15 minutes, stirring occasionally. Stir in the garlic and continue cooking until the onions are pale golden and very soft, about 10 minutes more.

3   Add the remaining ½ cup olive oil. Stir in the bell peppers, zucchini, and drained eggplant. Cover and cook until the vegetables are slightly softened, about 5 minutes, stirring once or twice. Stir in the tomatoes, increase the heat to high, and bring the mixture to a boil. Reduce the heat to low and simmer the sauce very gently until the vegetables have succumbed to the heat and become very tender, about 1 hour. As the samfaina cooks, only little bubbles should burst across its surface. If the mixture becomes too thick, stir in a little water so the vegetables have room to bathe. Remove the pan from the heat and stir in the pimentón.

EL CONSELL: You can make the samfaina ahead of time. Let it cool to room temperature, then store in small airtight containers in the refrigerator for up to 1 week or in the freezer for up to 3 months.

CIGRONS AMB ESPINACS
STEWED CHICKPEAS WITH SPINACH

Dried beans are a Catalan staple. I never even saw canned beans until I came to the United States, though they will work fine in this recipe. Mashing a few chickpeas into the garlic, parsley, and pine nut *picada* helps give the stew more body. I also like to add dried currants, which is the only change here from any Catalan grandmother's version of the dish. For a satisfying meal in the cooler months, pair this dish with Grilled Lamb Chops with Pedro Ximénez Vinegar (page 185).

1 tablespoon extra-virgin olive oil

1 tablespoon vegetable oil

1 slice day-old bread, crusts removed

4 garlic cloves, peeled

2 tablespoons pine nuts

¼ cup chopped fresh curly parsley

4 cups cooked or canned chickpeas

½ cup Sofregit (page 34) or store-bought sofrito

2 cups Vegetable Stock (page 35) or store-bought vegetable stock

5 ounces baby spinach

¼ cup dried currants

Pimentón (smoked paprika), for serving

1   In a large saucepan or stockpot, heat the oils over medium heat. When the oil is shimmering, add the bread and toast until it is golden brown and crisp on both sides, about 5 minutes, turning once. Remove to a plate. Add the garlic, pine nuts, and parsley to the hot oil and cook until the garlic is browned and the parsley is crisp, about 3 minutes, stirring to prevent burning. Remove the mixture to a plate or cutting board, reserving the oil in the saucepan.

2   Crumble the fried bread into a mortar. Use a pestle to pound the bread into fine crumbs, then mash in the reserved garlic, pine nuts, parsley, and 5 chickpeas to create a thick green picada paste. Set aside.

3   Return the saucepan with the reserved oil to high heat. When the oil is shimmering, add the picada, chickpeas, sofregit, and stock. Bring to a boil, then stir in the spinach and cook until it is wilted, about 5 minutes. Stir in the currants and cook until the currants are plump and the broth has thickened to a sauce, about 10 minutes. Sprinkle with pimentón and serve immediately.

EL CONSELL: If you have a few tablespoons of picada (Pounded Garlic and Parsley, page 29) made ahead, you can use it in place of the fried version made here.

If you want to turn this into a heartier meal, fry 4 eggs gently and lay them over the stewed greens and chickpeas so the runny yolk enhances the broth.

AMANIDA DE TOMÀQUET AMB FORMATGE DE CABRA

TEXAS PEACH AND TOMATO SALAD WITH GOAT CHEESE

SERVES 4 TO 6

AS A FIRST COURSE

OR TAPA

I love to make this salad when fresh tomato season knocks at the door. When I lived in San Francisco, we would get beautiful cases of heirloom tomatoes in all sorts of colors and shapes. Now that I'm in Texas, I add peaches to the mix, since I can find great ones in Austin. This salad is the perfect way to celebrate the excellent twelve-year-old vinegar from the Pedro Ximénez grape (see page 184) in the same simple way I would pull it together during the summertime in Vilafranca.

3 tablespoons extra-virgin olive oil

1 tablespoon PX vinegar or balsamic vinegar

1 tablespoon pitted and very finely chopped oil-cured black olives

2 pounds heirloom tomatoes, cut into bite-size pieces

1 pound peaches (about 3), cut into bite-size pieces

Kosher salt and freshly ground black pepper

1 tablespoon thinly sliced fresh basil leaves

3 ounces cold soft goat cheese

1   In a large bowl, whisk together the oil, vinegar, and olives. Add the tomatoes and peaches, season with salt and pepper, and toss gently to coat.

2   Divide the mixture among plates. Scatter over the basil and finely crumble the goat cheese on top. Spoon over any remaining vinaigrette from the bowl and serve.

PAELLES, ARROSSOS, I FIDEUS

PAELLA, RICE, AND NOODLES

A paella pan hangs in every Catalan kitchen, shiny with oil, ready for its next calling. The contents of the pan change with each cook and each season, like a dance changing with each partner and melody. For paella, the pan usually fills with the floral aroma and sunny color of saffron as the hot metal creates the prized *socarrat*, a deliciously crispy—almost burnt—layer of rice on the bottom. In other *arrossos*, or rice dishes, the pan serves as a cradle for a soupier dish with fat grains of rice plumped in savory broth among various meats and vegetables. And in *fideus*, the pan performs triple-duty by toasting angel-hair pasta directly over a flame, simmering it in aromatic broth, and then completing the dance in the warm embrace of a hot oven.

TIPS FOR PERFECT PAELLA

When I was nineteen or twenty, I returned from Chicago to Spain to fulfill my military duties. They sent me to Salamanca in the northwest, and I was broke. But I learned that good sofregit, some Spanish rice, and decent broth are all you need to make good paella. In fact, if you add too many other elements, they become *retallons (tropezones)*, little bits that cause your mouth to trip as it tries to taste the rice itself. Some people seem to like chorizo in paella, but Catalans would never do that—it gets in the way. Rice, stock, and sofregit. That is what you should taste in paella.

THE PAN: Cook with either a paella pan or a cast-iron skillet. I prefer carbon steel pans because they create the best *soccarat*. Pick one that is just big enough to hold the amount of rice you want to cook. The rice should never be more than 1 inch deep in the pan as it cooks. See the chart on the facing page for reference, and see page 27 for tips on caring for a paella pan.

THE RICE: Short- to medium-grain Spanish rice works best for paella. Most Catalan cooks prefer the bomba variety because it absorbs about three times its volume in liquid (and flavor) yet always stays white and chewy inside when cooked. "Extra" is the highest grade, with no broken grains, and is a common choice among the Catalan cooks I know. At my restaurant Barlata, we use a brand of bomba extra called Montsià. You could also use the Bahía variety or almost any other medium- to short-grain Spanish rice. Though I hate to admit it, if you're in a pinch, even Italian Arborio rice will work.

THE PREP: Make ahead whatever you can, such as sofregit (page 34), *picada* (Pounded Garlic and Parsley, page 29), and the stock (page 35). With these items in the freezer, you'll be ready to create deep flavors in what is otherwise a humble rice dish.

THE FLAME: Try to cook on a heat source wide enough to cover the entire bottom of the pan you are using, which will help the rice toast evenly. It may be helpful to use a heat diffuser and to rotate the pan for even cooking.

THE SAFFRON: Look for dark red saffron rather than yellow saffron. I believe saffron from Iran and Afghanistan is the most pure. It is also less expensive than Spanish saffron.

THE STOCK: Be sure to use good-quality stock, preferably homemade (see page 35). As a last resort, you could rehydrate a good-quality stock concentrate such as Better Than Bouillon. Either way, be sure the stock is simmering. Hot stock is crucial to cooking paella properly because, as the saying goes, the rice doesn't wait—not even for the stock to heat up as you cook. Keep a saucepan of stock simmering near your paella pan. When it is ladled in, the stock should immediately bubble and scream, boiling furiously around the edges. Ladle it slowly into the center of the pan at first. Keep in mind that you may not use all the stock called for in a recipe. It all depends on your pan, the heat level, the rice, and the other ingredients. The dance of how paella cooks changes each time and is more of an art than a precise science. Ultimately, it takes some practice and a "feel" for when the rice is just tender on top of the paella and crisped up into a deliciously caramelized *soccarat* on the bottom.

PAN SIZE	RICE	STOCK	SERVING SIZE
8- to 9-inch	⅔ cup	2½ to 3½ cups	1 as a main, 2 as a tapa
10-inch	¾ cup	3 to 4 cups	2 as a main, 4 as a tapa
12-inch	1 cup	4 to 5 cups	4 as a main, 6 as a tapa
13- to 14-inch	1¼ cups	5 to 6 cups	6 as a main, 8 as a tapa
15-inch	1⅓ cups	5½ to 6½ cups	8 as a main, 10 as a tapa

PAELLA DE LA CASA
HOUSE PAELLA

In Spain, rice dishes are more about the rice than the add-ins. But in America, more is more, so this paella is filled to the brim with chicken, shrimp, clams, mussels, squid, and chorizo. The idea here is to add whatever you want. I am a firm believer that the beauty of paella is that it can be changed to suit your preferences, depending on the season, where you are, and who is eating it. This version is for my American friends.

About 5 cups Chicken Stock (page 35) or store-bought chicken stock

2 small garlic cloves, peeled

2 pinches of pure saffron (about ¼ teaspoon)

⅛ teaspoon plus ½ teaspoon kosher salt

6 tablespoons fresh curly parsley leaves

2½ tablespoons extra-virgin olive oil

1 small (3-ounce) boneless, skinless chicken thigh, chopped

¼ cup squid bodies, sliced into rings and tentacles

2 tablespoons finely chopped smoked, cured chorizo sausage

1 cup Spanish rice, such as bomba

¼ cup Sofregit (page 34) or store-bought sofrito

½ teaspoon pimentón (smoked paprika)

¼ teaspoon freshly ground black pepper

6 littleneck or Manila clams, scrubbed

6 mussels, scrubbed and debearded

4 medium tail-on shrimp (21/25 count), peeled and deveined

2 tablespoons frozen peas, thawed

2 tablespoons fresh thin green beans or haricots verts, cut into ½-inch pieces

4 small lemon wedges, for serving

1   In a medium saucepan, bring the stock to a gentle simmer over medium heat.

2   Make a *picada* by mashing the garlic, saffron, and ⅛ teaspoon of the salt to a fine paste in a mortar with a pestle. Gradually add the parsley leaves, mashing each addition completely before adding more, until you have a green paste. Stir in ½ tablespoon of the olive oil and a few spoonfuls of warm stock to loosen the mixture so it is just runny enough to slowly drip from the spoon.

3   In a 12-inch paella pan, heat the remaining 2 tablespoons oil over medium-high heat. When the oil is shimmering, add the chicken, squid, and chorizo. Cook, tossing, until the chicken and squid begin to shrink and turn opaque, 1 to 2 minutes. Stir in the rice until it is shiny with oil, then add the picada, sofregit, pimentón, black pepper, and remaining ½ teaspoon salt. Add about 3 cups of hot stock to the pan, shaking it to settle and loosen any rice clusters as the stock begins to boil. Only shake the rice at this point; if stirred, it will become sticky.

(recipe continues)

4   Reduce the heat to medium-low and simmer the paella until about 80 percent of the liquid is absorbed, about 10 minutes. When most of the liquid is absorbed, the rice will start to sizzle a bit, almost as if it is asking you for another drink. At that point, add about 1 cup more stock by drizzling it around the edge of the pan so the stock seeps from the pan edge to the center.

5   Arrange the clams and mussels around the outer edge of the pan, and bury the shrimp throughout the rice. Simmer until about 80 percent of the liquid is absorbed and the rice starts to sizzle again, 5 to 6 minutes more. Drizzle about 1 cup more stock around the pan edge, and scatter the peas and green beans over the rice. Continue to simmer the rice until it is just beginning to become tender, 5 to 6 minutes more. At this point, the shrimp should be pink, the vegetables cooked through, and the clams and mussels should be open. Test the rice by taking a bite. The paella is done when the rice is plump, glossy, and tender on the surface with a firm white center when bitten into.

6   The edge of the paella pan should also have a dark rim of oily starch, which is a good sign of the crispy *socarrat* below. To test the socarrat, use a spoon to scrape the bottom of the paella pan. If the spoon doesn't move through the rice but instead the rice is firm and the pan moves, then the socarrat has begun to form. When the socarrat has begun, rotate the pan for even browning. The rice will talk to you as it cooks; the crackle will get faster as the rice dries out, then it will go silent when the socarrat is finished forming. Your nose will tell you if it's beginning to burn; just add a spoonful of stock to the scorching spot if so.

7   Serve the paella at the center of the table with spoons for guests to serve themselves and lemon wedges for squeezing.

EL CONSELL: For a nice touch, drizzle the paella with a little Pimentón Oil (page 147) and a roasted red pepper puree before bringing the paella to the table. To make the puree, simply mash some roasted red pepper, salt, and extra-virgin olive oil in a mortar with a pestle until smooth and pourable.

PAELLA DE LA BARCELONETA
SEAFOOD PAELLA

Barceloneta is a neighborhood in Barcelona bordering the water. For years, the railroad track separated the beach from the city and, when I was growing up, Barceloneta was a ghetto for fishermen, vagrants, and warehouses. Yet, the *chiringuitos* (beachside restaurants) on this strip of beach served the most famous seafood in the area. In 1992, after the Summer Olympic Games in Barcelona, this neighborhood changed into a vibrant destination for tourists and chic locals, while still remaining a humble neighborhood, at least in part. This recipe was inspired by my *bon amic* and well-known Catalan chef Quim Marquès, who serves something similar at his waterfront Barceloneta restaurant called Suquet de l'Amirall.

About 5 cups Fish Stock (page 35) or store-bought fish stock

2 small garlic cloves, peeled

2 pinches of pure saffron (about ¼ teaspoon)

⅛ teaspoon plus ½ teaspoon kosher salt

6 tablespoons fresh parsley leaves

2½ tablespoons extra-virgin olive oil

¼ cup squid bodies, sliced into rings and tentacles

2 ounces firm white fish, such as monkfish or snapper, cut into 1-inch pieces

1 cup Spanish rice, such as bomba

¼ cup Sofregit (page 34) or store-bought sofrito

½ teaspoon Caramelized Onion Marmalade (page 29)

½ teaspoon pimentón (smoked paprika)

¼ teaspoon freshly ground black pepper

4 littleneck or cherrystone clams, scrubbed

4 medium tail-on shrimp (21/25 count), peeled and deveined

2 tablespoons frozen peas, thawed

4 small lemon wedges, for serving

1 In a medium saucepan, bring the stock to a gentle simmer over medium heat.

2 Meanwhile, make a *picada* by mashing the garlic, saffron, and ⅛ teaspoon of the salt to a fine paste in a mortar with a pestle. Gradually add in the parsley leaves, mashing each addition completely before adding more, until you have a green paste. Stir in ½ tablespoon of the olive oil and a few spoonfuls of warm stock to loosen the mixture so it is just runny enough to slowly drip from the spoon.

3 In a 12-inch paella pan, heat the remaining 2 tablespoons oil over high heat. When the oil is shimmering, add the squid and fish. Cook, tossing, until the squid and fish begin to shrink and turn opaque, 1 to 2 minutes.

(recipe continues)

Stir in the rice until it is shiny with oil, then add the sofregit, onion marmalade, pimentón, black pepper, and remaining ½ teaspoon salt. Add about 3 cups of hot stock and the picada to the pan, shaking it to settle and loosen any rice clusters as the stock begins to boil. Only shake the rice at this point; if stirred, it will become sticky.

4   Reduce the heat to medium-low and simmer the paella until about 80 percent of the liquid is absorbed, about 10 minutes. When most of the liquid is absorbed, the rice will start to sizzle a bit, almost as if it is asking you for another drink. At that point, add about 1 cup more stock by drizzling it around the edge of the pan so the stock seeps from the pan edge to the center.

5   Arrange the clams around the outer edge of the pan, and bury the shrimp throughout the rice. Simmer until about 80 percent of the liquid is absorbed and the rice starts to sizzle again, 5 to 6 minutes more. Drizzle about 1 cup more stock around the pan edge and scatter the peas over the rice. Continue to simmer the rice until it is just beginning to become tender, 5 to 6 minutes more. At this point, the shrimp should be pink, the peas cooked through, and the clams should be open. Test the rice by taking a bite. The paella is done when the rice is plump, glossy, and tender on the surface with a firm white center when bitten into.

6   The edge of the paella pan should now have a dark rim of oily starch, which is a good sign of the crispy *socarrat* below. To test the socarrat, use a spoon to scrape the bottom of the paella pan. If the spoon doesn't move through the rice but instead the rice is firm and the pan moves, then the socarrat has begun to form. When the socarrat has begun, rotate the pan for even browning. The rice will talk to you as it cooks; the crackle will get faster as the rice dries out, then it will go silent when the socarrat is finished forming. Your nose will tell you if it's beginning to burn; just add a spoonful of stock to the scorching spot if so.

7   Serve the paella at the center of the table with spoons for guests to serve themselves and lemon wedges for squeezing.

PAELLA VALENCIANA
VALENCIAN PAELLA

Paella is said to come from Valencia, which is very near where rice was first planted by the Moors in Spain's swampy Albufera region. According to legend, the first paella was cooked over an open fire made with olive and orange tree branches and included readily available meats like rabbit, chicken, and even foraged snails in combination with dried beans. In Spain, I would find *bajoqueta de ferradura* or *garrofó* beans to make this Valencian paella really authentic. But frozen and thawed baby lima beans make a readily available substitute.

About 5 cups Chicken Stock (page 35) or store-bought chicken stock

2 sprigs fresh rosemary

2 pinches of pure saffron (about ¼ teaspoon)

2 tablespoons extra-virgin olive oil

1 small (3-ounce) boneless, skinless chicken thigh, chopped

3 ounces boneless rabbit loin meat, cut into 1-inch pieces

1 cup Spanish rice, such as bomba

¼ cup Sofregit (page 34) or store-bought sofrito

¼ cup frozen baby lima beans, thawed

1   In a medium saucepan, combine the stock, rosemary, and saffron and bring to a gentle simmer over medium heat.

2   In a 12-inch paella pan, heat the oil over medium-high heat until hot. When the oil is shimmering, add the chicken and rabbit and cook until the pieces of meat begin to shrink and turn opaque, 1 to 2 minutes, tossing frequently. Stir in the rice until it is shiny with oil, then stir in the sofregit and beans. Add about 3 cups of hot stock, shaking the pan to settle and loosen any rice clusters as the stock begins to boil. Only shake the rice at this point; if stirred, it will become sticky.

3   Reduce the heat to medium-low and simmer the paella until about 80 percent of the liquid is absorbed, about 10 minutes. When most of the liquid is absorbed, the rice will start to sizzle a bit, almost as if it is asking you for another drink. At that point, add about 1 cup more stock by drizzling it around the edge of the pan so the stock seeps from the pan edge to the center.

4 Simmer until about 80 percent of the liquid is absorbed and the rice starts to sizzle again, 5 to 6 minutes more. Drizzle about 1 cup more stock around the pan edge, and continue to simmer the rice until it is just beginning to become tender, 5 to 6 minutes more. Test the rice by taking a bite. The paella is done when the rice is plump, glossy, and tender on the surface with a firm white center when bitten into.

5 The edge of the paella pan should now have a dark rim of oily starch, which is a good sign of the crispy *socarrat* below. To test the socarrat, use a spoon to scrape the bottom of the paella pan. If the spoon doesn't move through the rice but instead the rice is firm and the pan moves, then the socarrat has begun to form. When the socarrat has begun, rotate the pan for even browning. The rice will talk to you as it cooks; the crackle will get faster as the rice dries out, then it will go silent when the socarrat is finished forming. Your nose will tell you if it's beginning to burn; just add a spoonful of stock to the scorching spot if so.

6 Remove the rosemary sprigs. Serve the paella at the center of the table with spoons for guests to serve themselves.

PAELLA DE L'HORTA

VEGETARIAN PAELLA

I have many fond memories of grilling in Vilafranca. When I was a boy, grilling vegetables over collected vine trimmings was a neighborhood activity that gathered all of the mothers in town. They would cradle the produce in their aprons and empty the hammocked produce directly into the glowing embers (see page 92 for more on this story). If you like, you could grill the vegetables over a wood or charcoal fire because it will deepen the flavor of the paella—which always reminds me of home.

About 5 cups Vegetable Stock (page 35) or store-bought vegetable stock

1 garlic clove, peeled

2 pinches of pure saffron (about ¼ teaspoon)

2 ounces dried porcini or shiitake mushrooms

1 cup boiling water

2 tablespoons plus 1 teaspoon extra-virgin olive oil

¼ cup halved and thinly sliced yellow onion

¼ cup finely chopped red bell pepper

2 asparagus stalks, trimmed and cut on the diagonal into ½-inch pieces

3 ounces sliced mixed fresh mushrooms, such as oyster, portobello, and shiitake

1 cup Spanish rice, such as bomba

¼ cup Sofregit (page 34) or store-bought sofrito

2 teaspoons Caramelized Onion Marmalade (page 29)

1 teaspoon mashed roasted red pepper

½ teaspoon kosher salt

½ teaspoon pimentón (smoked paprika)

¼ teaspoon freshly ground black pepper

2 tablespoons frozen peas, thawed

1 ounce thin green beans or haricots verts, cut into ½-inch lengths

1 tablespoon pine nuts, toasted

2 tablespoons dried currants or raisins

½ cup (½ ounce) baby arugula

¼ teaspoon cava vinegar or champagne vinegar

1 tablespoon Allioli (page 32) or store-bought aioli, for serving

1   In a medium saucepan, bring the stock to a gentle simmer over medium heat.

2   Make a *picada* by mashing the garlic and saffron to a fine paste in a mortar with a pestle. Mix in a few spoonfuls of warm stock to dissolve the saffron paste and loosen the mixture so it is just runny enough to slowly drip from the spoon.

3   Place the dried mushrooms in a small heatproof bowl and pour the boiling water over them. Let stand until the mushrooms swell significantly and the water is dark and fragrant, about 15 minutes. Pluck out the mushrooms, squeezing them to fully extract the liquid. Discard the rehydrated mushrooms (I use them only to make a flavorful mushroom stock).

(recipe continues)

4 Meanwhile, in a 12-inch paella pan, heat 2 tablespoons of the oil over medium-high heat. When the oil is shimmering, add the onion, red bell pepper, asparagus, and fresh mushrooms. Cook until the vegetables begin to sizzle and brown, 1 to 2 minutes, tossing frequently. Stir in the rice until it is shiny with oil, then add the sofregit, onion marmalade, roasted red pepper, salt, pimentón, and black pepper. Pour the reserved mushroom soaking liquid through a small strainer to catch any grit, straining the liquid directly into the pan. Add the picada and about 3 cups of hot stock to the pan, shaking it to settle and loosen any rice clusters as the stock begins to boil. Only shake the rice at this point; if stirred, it will become sticky.

5 Reduce the heat to medium-low and simmer the paella until about 80 percent of the liquid is absorbed, about 10 minutes. When most of the liquid is absorbed, the rice will start to sizzle a bit, almost as if it is asking you for another drink. At that point, add about 1 cup more stock by drizzling it around the edge of the pan so the stock seeps from the pan edge to the center.

6 Simmer until about 80 percent of the liquid is absorbed and the rice starts to sizzle again, 5 to 6 minutes more. Drizzle about 1 cup more stock around the pan edge, and scatter the peas and green beans over the paella. Continue to simmer the rice until it is just beginning to become tender, 5 to 6 minutes more. Test the rice by taking a bite. The paella is done when the rice is plump, glossy, and tender on the surface with a firm white center when bitten into. Sprinkle the rice with the pine nuts and currants.

7 The edge of the paella pan should now have a dark rim of oily starch, which is a good sign of the crispy *socarrat* below. To test the socarrat, use a spoon to scrape the bottom of the paella pan. If the spoon doesn't move through the rice but instead the rice is firm and the pan moves, then the socarrat has begun to form. When the socarrat has begun, rotate the pan for even browning. The rice will talk to you as it cooks; the crackle will get faster as the rice dries out, then it will go silent when the socarrat is finished forming. Your nose will tell you if it's beginning to burn; just add a spoonful of stock to the scorching spot if so.

8 In a small bowl, toss the arugula with the remaining 1 teaspoon oil and the vinegar, and season with salt and pepper. Pile the greens around the edge of the paella like a wreath. Spoon the allioli onto the center of the paella.

9 Serve the paella at the center of the table with spoons for guests to serve themselves, stirring in the allioli only after the paella is on the table.

EL CONSELL: For a brunch dish, top this paella with a few runny fried eggs.

ARRÒS NEGRE
BLACK RICE IN SQUID INK BROTH

I serve my *arròs* a little juicier and creamier than my paella, a little like a risotto that hasn't been stirred. This version has an arresting black color and deep briny flavor from squid ink stirred into the broth. Even though *paellas* are named for their unique pan, arròs dishes are best cooked in paella pans as well. But you won't find paella's signature *socarrat* here—instead, a little reduced broth should bubble at the bottom of the pan as it is brought to the table.

About 5 cups Fish Stock (page 35) or store-bought fish stock

1 teaspoon to 1 tablespoon squid ink (see note)

1 small garlic clove, peeled

⅛ teaspoon plus ½ teaspoon kosher salt

6 tablespoons fresh curly parsley leaves

2½ tablespoons extra-virgin olive oil

¼ cup halved and thinly sliced white onion

¼ cup finely chopped red bell pepper

¼ cup squid bodies, sliced into rings and tentacles

2 ounces cuttlefish or squid steaks, cut into ½-inch pieces

1 cup Spanish rice, such as bomba

¼ cup Sofregit (page 34) or store-bought sofrito

½ teaspoon pimentón (smoked paprika)

¼ teaspoon freshly ground black pepper

4 cherrystone or littleneck clams, scrubbed

4 medium shrimp (21/25 count), peeled and deveined, tail left on

¼ cup frozen peas, thawed

2 tablespoons Allioli (page 32) or store-bought aioli, for serving

1 In a medium saucepan, combine the stock and enough squid ink to make a deep black broth that tastes strongly of the ocean. Bring to a gentle simmer over medium-low heat.

2 Meanwhile, make a *picada* by mashing the garlic and ⅛ teaspoon of the salt to a fine paste in a mortar with a pestle. Gradually add in the parsley leaves, mashing each addition completely before adding more, until you have a green paste. Stir in ½ tablespoon of the olive oil and set aside.

3 In a 12-inch paella pan, heat the remaining 2 tablespoons oil over medium heat. When the oil is shimmering, add the onion and bell pepper and cook until the vegetables are softened, 5 to 7 minutes, stirring occasionally. Increase the heat to medium-high and add the squid and cuttlefish. Cook until the squid and cuttlefish begin to shrink and turn opaque, 1 to 2 minutes, tossing frequently. Stir in the rice until it is shiny with oil, then add the picada,

(recipe continues)

sofregit, pimentón, remaining ½ teaspoon salt, and the black pepper. Add about 3 cups of warm stock to the pan, shaking the pan to settle and loosen any rice clusters as the stock begins to boil. Only shake the rice at this point; if stirred, it will become sticky.

4   Simmer the rice over medium-high heat until about 80 percent of the liquid is absorbed, about 10 minutes. When most of the liquid is absorbed, the rice will start to sizzle a bit, almost as if it is asking you for another drink. At that point, add about 1 cup more stock by drizzling it around the edge of the pan so the stock seeps from the pan edge to the center.

5   Arrange the clams around the outer edge of the pan, and bury the shrimp throughout the rice. Simmer until about 80 percent of the liquid is absorbed and the rice starts to sizzle again, 5 to 6 minutes more. Drizzle about 1 cup more stock around the pan edge, and scatter the peas over the rice. Continue to simmer the rice until it is just beginning to become tender, 5 to 6 minutes more. At this point, the clams should be open and the shrimp should be pink. The arròs is done when the rice is plump, glossy, and firm with a dense white center when bitten into and there is still some broth in the pan. To test it, use a metal spoon to push the rice from the edge of the pan; the broth should pool into the empty spot.

6   Spoon the allioli onto the center of the arròs. Serve at the center of the table with spoons for guests to serve themselves, stirring in the allioli only after the arròs is on the table.

EL CONSELL: Look for squid ink in bottles at an Asian market. You may need more or less, depending on its strength.

For an optional finishing touch here, double the amount of picada you make for this recipe and set half of it aside. Or if you've made up some picada ahead of time, use about 1 teaspoon picada or Pounded Garlic and Parsley (page 29). Mix the reserved picada with 1 tablespoon olive oil and a pinch of lemon zest. Spoon the mixture over the arròs before serving and before stirring in the allioli. Try this finishing touch on *arròs blanc* (Rice with Seafood, page 126) and *arròs a la caçadora* (Hunter's Rice, page 128) as well.

ROSSEJAT
ROASTED RICE PAELLA

Rossejat, like many Catalan rice dishes, started as a fisherman's dish. It is probably the quickest and most traditional version of all of the paellas because it comes together with the fewest ingredients. It is essentially a roasted rice dish—almost like Spanish fried rice. The grains get crunchy and flavorful without the need for expensive saffron or even a paella pan. Because the recipe is so simple, it is important to use a very concentrated stock made with shrimp heads, which deepen the savory taste of the rice.

4 large shell-on, head-on shrimp (16/20 count)

2 tablespoons vegetable oil

1 tablespoon extra-virgin olive oil

2 medium carrots, peeled and sliced

1 celery rib, sliced

1 medium leek, halved lengthwise and thinly sliced

2 garlic cloves, smashed and peeled

¼ cup Sofregit (page 34) or store-bought sofrito

¼ teaspoon plus ⅛ teaspoon pimentón (smoked paprika)

About 5 cups Fish Stock (page 35) or store-bought fish stock

1 cup Spanish rice, such as bomba

⅛ teaspoon kosher salt

Pinch of freshly ground black pepper

2 tablespoons Allioli (page 32) or store-bought aioli, for serving

1   Pull the shrimp heads away from their bodies and set them aside.

2   Mix together the oils. In a medium saucepan, heat 1 tablespoon of the mixed oil over medium heat. When the oil is shimmering, add the carrots, celery, leek, and garlic. Cook until the leek is wilted and beginning to brown, about 5 minutes. Stir in the sofregit, ¼ teaspoon of the pimentón, the stock, and shrimp heads. Increase the heat to high and bring the liquid to a boil, then reduce the heat to low and simmer gently for 10 minutes. Using a fine-mesh strainer to scoop out the solids, leave the stock to simmer on the stove while you prepare the rest of the paella (discard the solids). As it simmers, the stock should reduce in volume and become very concentrated in flavor.

3   In a 12- to 14-inch cast-iron skillet, heat the remaining 2 tablespoons mixed oil over high heat. When the oil is shimmering, add the shrimp bodies and sear until the shells just start to turn pink, about 2 minutes, turning once. Remove to a plate. Stir the rice into the oil in the pan and cook until the grains turn golden brown and smell like popcorn, about 3 minutes. Stir in the salt, the remaining ⅛ teaspoon pimentón, the black pepper, and about 3 cups of hot stock, shaking the pan to settle and loosen any rice clusters as the stock begins to boil. Only shake the rice at this point; if stirred, it will become sticky.

4   Simmer the rice quickly over medium heat until about 80 percent of the liquid is absorbed, 8 to 10 minutes. When most of the liquid is absorbed, the rice will start to sizzle a bit, almost as if it is asking you for another drink. At that point, add about 1 cup more stock by drizzling it around the edge of the pan so the stock seeps from the pan edge to the center.

5   Simmer until about 80 percent of the liquid is absorbed and the rice starts to sizzle again, 5 to 6 minutes more. Drizzle about 1 cup more stock around the pan edge, and bury the shrimp throughout the rice. Continue to simmer until the shrimp are bright pink and the rice is just beginning to become tender, 5 to 6 minutes more. Test the rice by taking a bite. The rossejat is done when the rice is plump, glossy, and tender on the surface with a firm white center when bitten into.

6   The edge of the paella pan should now have a dark rim of oily starch, which is a good sign of the crispy *socarrat* below. To test the socarrat, use a spoon to scrape the bottom of the paella pan. If the spoon doesn't move through the rice but instead the rice is firm and the pan moves, then the socarrat has begun to form. When the socarrat has begun, rotate the pan for even browning. The rice will talk to you as it cooks; the crackle will get faster as the rice dries out, then it will go silent when the socarrat is finished forming. Your nose will tell you if it's beginning to burn; just add a spoonful of stock to the scorching spot if so.

7   Spoon the allioli onto the center of the rossejat. Serve at the center of the table with spoons for guests to serve themselves, stirring in the allioli only after the rossejat is on the table.

ARRÒS BLANC
RICE WITH SEAFOOD

If you're out of saffron, here's the perfect rice dish. I like to make it with lots of seafood and call it *blanc* to contrast with my dark arròs, Black Rice in Squid Ink Broth (page 119). Use any odd pieces of frozen seafood you have in your freezer. I usually have some shrimp and salt cod in my freezer, but this is the sort of dish I will improvise when my kitchen is down to the bare-bones staples and I want to make something that tastes like the sea. Just be sure to soak the cod the night before to remove the excess salt.

About 5 cups Fish Stock (page 35) or store-bought fish stock

1 small garlic clove, peeled

⅛ teaspoon plus ½ teaspoon kosher salt

6 tablespoons fresh curly parsley leaves

2½ tablespoons extra-virgin olive oil

¼ cup halved and thinly sliced small white onion

¼ cup finely chopped red bell pepper

2 ounces salt cod, desalted (page 157), drained, and shredded into bite-size pieces

3 ounces firm white fish, such as monkfish or snapper, cut into 1-inch pieces

1 cup Spanish rice, such as bomba

¼ cup Sofregit (page 34) or store-bought sofrito

½ teaspoon pimentón (smoked paprika)

¼ teaspoon freshly ground black pepper

4 medium shrimp (21/25 count), peeled and deveined, tails left on

2 tablespoons Allioli (page 32) or store-bought aioli, for serving

1   In a medium saucepan, bring the stock to a gentle simmer over medium heat.

2   Meanwhile, make a *picada* by mashing the garlic and ⅛ teaspoon of the salt to a fine paste in a mortar with a pestle. Gradually add in the parsley leaves, mashing each addition completely before adding more, until you have a green paste. Stir in ½ tablespoon of the olive oil and set aside.

3   In a 12-inch paella pan, heat the remaining 2 tablespoons oil over medium heat. When the oil is shimmering, add the onion and bell pepper and cook until softened, 5 to 7 minutes, stirring occasionally. Increase the heat to medium-high and add the salt cod and fish. Cook until the fish begins to shrink and turn opaque, 1 to 2 minutes, tossing frequently.

Stir in the rice until it is shiny with oil, then add the picada, sofregit, pimentón, black pepper, and remaining ½ teaspoon salt. Add about 3 cups of warm stock to the pan, shaking it to settle and loosen any rice clusters as the stock begins to boil. Only shake the rice at this point; if stirred, it will become sticky.

4   Simmer the rice over medium-high heat until about 80 percent of the liquid is absorbed, about 10 minutes. When most of the liquid is absorbed, the rice will start to sizzle a bit, almost as if it is asking you for another drink. At that point, add about 1 cup more stock by drizzling it around the edge of the pan so the stock seeps from the pan edge to the center.

5   Bury the shrimp throughout the rice and simmer until about 80 percent of the liquid is absorbed and the rice starts to sizzle again, 5 to 6 minutes more. Drizzle about 1 cup more stock around the pan edge and continue to simmer the rice until it is just beginning to become tender, 5 to 6 minutes more. At this point, the shrimp should be pink. The *arròs* is done when the rice is plump, glossy, and firm with a dense white center when bitten into and there is still some broth in the pan. To test it, use a metal spoon to push the rice from the edge of the pan; the broth should pool into the empty spot.

6   Spoon the allioli onto the center of the arròs. Serve at the center of the table with spoons for guests to serve themselves, stirring in the allioli only after the arròs is on the table.

ARRÒS A LA CAÇADORA
HUNTER'S RICE

SERVES 2
AS A MAIN DISH
OR 4 TO SHARE

While many of my favorite paellas are full of seafood and remind me of summer beach days, this dish is the kind you would make inland. It's called Hunter's Rice because it is full of the hearty flavors and aromas of fall and winter such as mushrooms and rabbit. Porcini mushrooms are my favorite to use here because their woodsy aroma reminds me of the Pyrenees mountains.

About 5 cups Beef Stock (page 35) or store-bought beef stock

2 ounces dried porcini or shiitake mushrooms, broken into small pieces

1 cup boiling water

1 small garlic clove, peeled

⅛ teaspoon plus ½ teaspoon kosher salt

6 tablespoons fresh curly parsley leaves

2½ tablespoons extra-virgin olive oil

3 ounces thinly sliced pancetta, chopped

1 small (3-ounce) boneless, skinless chicken thigh, cut into pieces

2 ounces boneless rabbit loin meat, cut into 1-inch pieces (see note)

6 ounces sliced or chopped mixed fresh mushrooms, such as oyster, portobello, and shiitake

1 cup Spanish rice, such as bomba

¼ cup Sofregit (page 34) or store-bought sofrito

½ teaspoon pimentón (smoked paprika)

¼ teaspoon freshly ground black pepper

1 In a medium saucepan, bring the stock to a gentle simmer over medium heat.

2 Place the dried mushrooms in a small heatproof bowl and pour the boiling water over them. Let stand until the mushrooms swell significantly and the water is dark and fragrant, about 15 minutes. Pluck out the mushrooms, squeezing to extract the liquid. Rinse the mushrooms to remove any grit. Reserve the liquid and the mushrooms separately.

3 Meanwhile, make a *picada* by mashing the garlic and ⅛ teaspoon of the salt to a fine paste in a mortar with a pestle. Gradually add in the parsley leaves, mashing each addition completely before adding more, until you have a green paste. Stir in ½ tablespoon of the olive oil and set aside.

4   In a 12-inch paella pan, heat the remaining 2 tablespoons oil over high heat. When the oil is shimmering, stir in the pancetta and cook until the fat has rendered, about 2 minutes, stirring frequently. Add the chicken, rabbit, fresh mushrooms, and reserved soaked mushrooms. Cook until the rabbit and chicken begin to shrink and turn opaque, 1 to 2 minutes, tossing frequently. Stir in the rice until it is shiny with oil, then add the picada, sofregit, pimentón, black pepper, and remaining ½ teaspoon salt. Pour the reserved mushroom soaking liquid through a small strainer to catch any grit, straining the liquid directly into the pan. Add about 3 cups of warm stock to the pan, shaking it to settle and loosen any rice clusters as the stock begins to boil. Only shake the rice at this point; if stirred, it will become sticky.

5   Simmer the rice over medium-high heat until about 80 percent of the liquid is absorbed, about 10 minutes. When most of the liquid is absorbed, the rice will start to sizzle a bit, almost as if it is asking you for another drink. At that point, add about 1 cup more stock by drizzling it around the edge of the pan so the stock seeps from the pan edge to the center.

6   Simmer until about 80 percent of the liquid is absorbed and the rice starts to sizzle again, 5 to 6 minutes more. Drizzle about 1 cup more stock around the pan edge, and continue to simmer the rice until it is just beginning to become tender, 5 to 6 minutes more. The *arròs* is done when the rice is plump, glossy, and firm with a dense white center when bitten into and there is still some broth in the pan. To test it, use a metal spoon to push the rice from the edge of the pan; the broth should pool into the empty spot.

7   Serve at the center of the table with spoons for guests to serve themselves.

EL CONSELL: You could substitute the rabbit with any other meat such as quail or pork sausage.

ARRÒS AUSTIN

SMOKED RICE WITH PORK BELLY AND MUSHROOMS

About a year after moving to Austin, I had settled into the food scene and began to crave barbecue like a local. This recipe calls for smoking the rice briefly over smoldering hickory wood chips, a step that lends the dish the aromas of Texas. If you don't want to do it, skip that step, but I encourage you to try.

½ cup hickory wood chips

1 cup Spanish rice, such as bomba

About 5 cups Pork or Chicken Stock (page 35) or store-bought stock

2 ounces dried porcini or shiitake mushrooms, broken into pieces

1 cup boiling water

1 small garlic clove, peeled

⅛ teaspoon plus ½ teaspoon kosher salt

6 tablespoons curly parsley leaves

2½ tablespoons extra-virgin olive oil

¼ cup chopped Homemade Bacon (page 215), cansalada, or pancetta

6 ounces sliced mixed fresh mushrooms, such as oyster, portobello, and shiitake

½ cup Sofregit (page 34) or store-bought sofrito

½ teaspoon pimentón (smoked paprika)

¼ teaspoon freshly ground black pepper

½ cup Mustard Sauce (recipe follows)

1   Place the wood chips in foil, folding up the sides to create a sort of tray. Place the tray in the bottom of a medium saucepan and use a long-handled lighter to set the wood chips on fire (turn on your kitchen exhaust fan or do this outside). After the chips burn for 1 to 2 minutes, blow out the fire, leaving the chips to smolder. Pour the rice into a fine-mesh strainer and rest it on top of the pan, over the rising smoke. Cover everything tightly with foil and set aside until the rice takes on a smoky flavor, about 15 minutes.

2   Meanwhile, in a medium saucepan, bring the stock to a gentle simmer over medium heat. Place the dried mushrooms in a small heatproof bowl and pour the boiling water over them. Let stand until the mushrooms swell significantly and the water is dark and fragrant, about 15 minutes. Pluck out the mushrooms, squeezing to extract the liquid. Rinse the mushrooms to remove any grit. Reserve the liquid and mushrooms separately.

3   Meanwhile, make a *picada* by mashing the garlic and ⅛ teaspoon of the salt to a fine paste in a mortar with a pestle. Gradually add in the parsley leaves, mashing each addition completely before adding more, until you have a green paste. Stir in ½ tablespoon of the olive oil and set aside.

(recipe continues)

4   In a 12-inch paella pan, heat the remaining 2 tablespoons of oil over medium heat. When the oil is shimmering, add the bacon and fresh mushrooms and cook until the mushrooms have begun to wilt and release their liquid, 5 to 7 minutes, stirring occasionally. Stir in the smoked rice until it is shiny with oil, then add the picada, sofregit, pimentón, black pepper, and remaining ½ teaspoon salt. Stir the reserved soaked mushrooms into the pan. Pour the reserved mushroom soaking liquid through a small strainer to catch any grit, straining the liquid directly into the pan. Add about 3 cups hot stock, shaking it to settle and loosen any rice clusters as the stock begins to boil. Only shake the rice at this point; if stirred, it will become sticky.

5   Simmer the rice over medium-high heat until about 80 percent of the liquid is absorbed, about 10 minutes. When most of the liquid is absorbed, the rice will start to sizzle, almost as if it is asking you for another drink. At that point, add about 1 cup more stock by drizzling it around the edge of the pan.

6   Simmer until about 80 percent of the liquid is absorbed and the rice starts to sizzle again, 5 to 6 minutes more. Drizzle about 1 cup more stock around the pan edge, and continue to simmer the rice until it is just beginning to become tender, 5 to 6 minutes more. The *arròs* is done when the rice is plump, glossy, and firm with a dense white center when bitten into and there is still some broth in the pan. To test it, use a metal spoon to push the rice from the edge of the pan; the broth should pool into the empty spot.

7   Serve at the center of the table with spoons for guests to serve themselves. Serve the mustard sauce with a spoon for guests to drizzle over each serving of rice.

SALSA DE MOSTASSA
MUSTARD SAUCE

MAKES ½ CUP

6 tablespoons Dijon mustard
1 tablespoon Beef Stock (page 35) or store-bought beef stock
1 tablespoon honey
1½ teaspoons chopped fresh curly parsley
1½ teaspoons PX vinegar (see page 184) or aged balsamic vinegar

In a small saucepan, combine the mustard, stock, honey, parsley, and vinegar and heat over medium heat, stirring, until the sauce is blended and warmed through, about 5 minutes. Taste and, if necessary, season with salt and pepper.

FIDEUÀ

FIDEO NOODLE PAELLA

Fideuà is similar to paella but it is made with short toasted noodles called *fideus*, which you can find at Hispanic markets. You can also toast the noodles yourself as described here. The dish starts on the stovetop just like paella, but then it is finished in the oven. You can tell it is done when you look into the oven and the noodles are standing up—or *trempant*, as we say in Catalan, meaning "with an erection."

4 ounces store-bought toasted fideus or vermicelli pasta

3½ tablespoons extra-virgin olive oil

About 5 cups Fish Stock (page 35) or store-bought fish stock

1 small garlic clove, peeled

⅛ teaspoon plus ½ teaspoon kosher salt

6 tablespoons fresh curly parsley leaves

2 ounces firm white fish, such as monkfish or snapper, cut into 1-inch pieces

2 ounces cuttlefish or squid steaks, cut into ½-inch pieces

¼ cup squid bodies, sliced into rings and tentacles

¼ cup Sofregit (page 34) or store-bought sofrito

½ teaspoon Caramelized Onion Marmalade (page 29)

½ teaspoon pimentón (smoked paprika)

¼ teaspoon freshly ground black pepper

4 medium shrimp (21/25 count), peeled and deveined, tails left on

2 tablespoons frozen peas, thawed

2 tablespoons Allioli (page 32 or store-bought aioli, for serving

4 small lemon wedges, for serving

Pimentón Oil (optional; page 147), for serving

1   Preheat the oven to 350°F.

2   If you use vermicelli pasta, use your hands to break the pasta into 1-inch pieces over a large sheet pan. Drizzle 1 tablespoon of the oil over the pasta or fideus and toss to coat it well. Shake the noodles into a single layer, then toast in the oven until deep golden brown, 8 to 10 minutes, shaking the pan once or twice for even browning. Remove and let cool completely. This step can be done a day or two ahead.

3   Increase the oven temperature to 450°F.

4   In a medium saucepan, bring the stock to a gentle simmer over medium heat.

5   Meanwhile, make a *picada* by mashing the garlic and ⅛ teaspoon of the salt to a fine paste in a mortar with a pestle. Gradually add in the parsley, mashing each addition completely before adding more, until you have a green paste. Stir in ½ tablespoon of the olive oil and set aside.

(recipe continues)

6   In a 12-inch paella pan, heat the remaining 2 tablespoons oil over high heat. When the oil is shimmering, add the fish, cuttlefish, and squid. Cook until the fish begins to shrink and turn opaque, 1 to 2 minutes, tossing frequently. Stir in the toasted noodles until they are shiny with oil.

7   Add the picada, sofregit, onion marmalade, pimentón, black pepper, and remaining ½ teaspoon salt. Add about 3 cups of warm stock to the pan, shaking it to settle and loosen any noodle clusters as the stock begins to boil. Only shake the noodles at this point; if stirred, they will become sticky.

8   Simmer the fideos over medium heat until some stock is absorbed, about 10 minutes. Test the noodles for doneness—they should be about halfway cooked by now. If the noodles no longer have room to swim, add about 1 cup more stock. Continue to simmer the fideuà until only a thin layer of stock rests on top, up to 10 minutes more.

9   Bury the shrimp throughout the noodles and scatter the peas over the top. Transfer the pan to the oven and cook until the shrimp turn pink, all the stock has evaporated, and the crispy noodles stand up in the pan, 5 to 7 minutes.

10 Spoon the allioli onto the center of the noodles. Serve at the center of the table with spoons for guests to serve themselves and lemon wedges for squeezing. Stir the allioli into the noodles only after the dish is on the table. Drizzle with the pimentón oil.

DEL MAR A LA TAULA
FROM THE SEA
TO THE TABLE

Fish and fishing are a huge part of Catalan food culture. Each morning, fortunate fisherman auction fish on the beach or cart the fish to their wives to sell in the family shop. Every little town has multiple fish markets, and shopping at them is a daily ritual. Catalan seafood is abundant and viewed by locals as inexpensive, fresh fare on which a satisfying family meal can be built. Waiting in line at the fish market is part of the spectacle: Every shopper knows exactly what they want and how the fish should be broken down for the dish they plan to make. The fishmonger obliges with high standards to match the customer's high expectations: Sharp knives and exacting cuts on multiple varieties of freshly caught fish become part of the daily display.

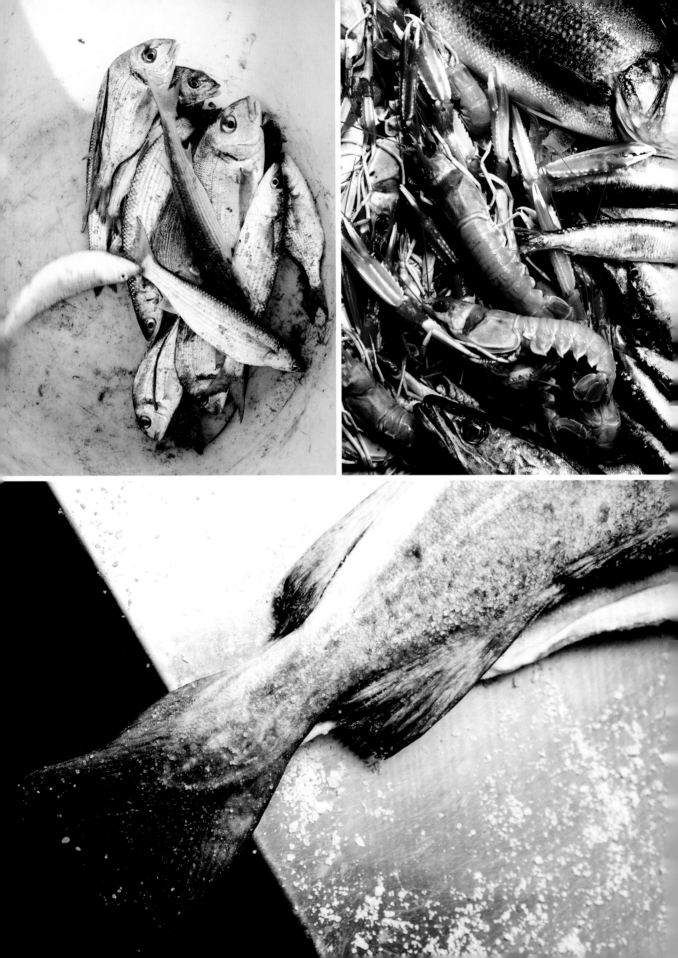

CALAMARS A LA SITGETANA
SQUID WITH ONIONS

In Catalonia, squid is usually cooked very quickly over high heat to keep it tender. To choose the freshest, most tender squid, be sure its freckled purple skin and ink sac are still intact. Store-bought calamari rings are often processed for cleaning, which toughens them before they even hit the pan. In Austin, I buy fresh squid from Central Market, and you should be able to do the same at your local reputable fish market.

1 tablespoon extra-virgin olive oil

1 tablespoon vegetable oil

1 pound squid bodies, sliced into rings and tentacles

3 medium yellow onions, halved and thinly sliced

4 to 5 garlic cloves, finely chopped

1 sprig fresh thyme

3 bay leaves

1 teaspoon fennel seeds

¼ cup dry white wine

1 cup Fish Stock (page 35) or store-bought fish stock

Chopped fresh curly parsley, for serving

1   In a large skillet, heat the oils over high heat. When the oil is shimmering, add the squid and cook until it shrinks and turns opaque, about 1 minute, tossing frequently. Use a slotted spoon to remove the squid to a small bowl, reserving the oil in the skillet over high heat. Add more oil if the pan seems dry.

2   Stir the onions into the hot oil, cover, and reduce the heat to low. Cook over low heat until the onions release their liquid, lose their crunch, and become translucent, about 15 minutes. Add the garlic and cook until tender, about 10 minutes more, stirring occasionally. Stir in the thyme, bay leaves, and fennel seeds. Pour in the wine, increase the heat to high, and bring to a boil. Reduce the heat to medium and simmer until the liquid is almost completely evaporated, about 5 minutes.

3   Add the stock and return the squid to the pan. Increase the heat to high and bring the stock to a boil, then reduce the heat to medium and simmer until the squid are tender and the liquid has reduced to a thin puddle at the bottom of the pan, about 5 minutes.

4   Discard the bay leaves and thyme and transfer the squid to a deep serving bowl. Scatter the parsley over the squid and serve in the center of the table.

EL CONSELL: For a classic variation on this dish, stir in ½ teaspoon *picada* (Pounded Garlic and Parsley, page 29) just before serving.

CLOÏSSES AMB VI BLANC

CLAMS IN WHITE WINE

SERVES 2
AS A MAIN DISH
OR 4 TO SHARE

A batch of sautéed clams comes together very quickly on a busy night and remains a favorite among Catalans. Bend this recipe to suit your taste. Add a pinch of pepper flakes to make it spicy, or stir in a tablespoon of romesco (Nut and Pepper Sauce, page 32) to make it creamy. In Catalonia, clams are prepared this way throughout the year and served with pieces of crunchy bread to nibble and a bottle of chilled cava to sip while waiting for the paella to come to the table.

1 tablespoon extra-virgin olive oil

1 tablespoon vegetable oil

4 garlic cloves, finely chopped

1 pound small clams, such as Manilas, scrubbed

¼ cup dry white wine

Kosher salt and freshly ground black pepper

2 tablespoons chopped fresh curly parsley

Crunchy bread, for serving

1   In a large Dutch oven, heat the oils over medium-high heat. When the oil is shimmering, add the garlic and cook until golden brown, about 2 minutes, stirring frequently.

2   Stir in the clams and wine, increase the heat to high, and bring to a boil. Then cover the pan, reduce the heat to medium-low, and cook until the clams have opened and released their juices, about 5 minutes. (Discard any clams that do not open.) Season with salt and pepper, then sprinkle with the parsley.

3   Serve in a bowl along with the bread and a separate bowl for the shells.

MUSCLOS AMB SOFREGIT

MUSSELS WITH SOFRITO

SERVES 2
AS A MAIN DISH
OR 4 TO SHARE

In Catalonia, mussels have to be *de la roca* (off the stone) or, even better, wild from the Catalan coast. Look for the smallest mussels you can find—they are usually sweetest and firmest. In the summertime, Catalans graze on mussels while waiting for seafood paella at *chiringuitos* or *guinguetes* (beachside restaurants). This recipe is the fastest and simplest one I make. Toss together some sofregit and mussels in a hot pan and it's done in a few minutes. The variations are truly endless: Add a bit of garlic with some cilantro, or use basil instead of tarragon. And this is the perfect place to use Homemade Bacon (page 215) in place of the pancetta, if you have some resting in your refrigerator.

1 tablespoon extra-virgin olive oil

1 tablespoon vegetable oil

2 ounces pancetta, chopped

4 garlic cloves, thinly sliced

1 tablespoon fresh tarragon leaves

¼ cup Sofregit (page 34) or store-bought sofrito

1 pound mussels, scrubbed and debearded

¼ cup dry white wine

¼ cup frozen peas, thawed

Kosher salt and freshly ground black pepper

1   In a medium Dutch oven, heat the oils over medium-high heat. When the oil is shimmering, add the pancetta and cook until the fat begins to render, about 5 minutes, stirring a few times. Stir in the garlic and tarragon, then the sofregit. Stir in the mussels and wine, increase the heat to high, and bring to a boil. Then cover the pan, reduce the heat to medium-low, and cook until the mussels open, about 5 minutes. (Discard any mussels that do not open.) Stir in the peas and season with salt and pepper.

2   Serve the mussels in a bowl along with an empty bowl for the shells.

POP A LA PALMA

OCTOPUS WITH CARAMELIZED ONION TOMATO SAUCE

Here's a riff on a dish served at Bar la Palma in Vilafranca, where my dad would take me as a kid. It became a family tradition to go there on August 30, right before we would join our neighbors in the Castellers de Vilafranca (human tower builders of Vilafranca) to build giant human towers in the center of town for the *festa major*, our annual celebration of the town's patron saint, Saint Fèlix. When I make this dish, it transports me home. To prolong the experience, I cook it one day and eat it the next, which also gives the flavors time to blend. To read more about the festivities surrounding Festa Major, see page 164.

½ cup extra-virgin olive oil

2 medium yellow onions, halved and thinly sliced

12 garlic cloves, peeled and halved

8 tentacles from a 4- to 6-pound octopus, cooked (see page 147) and sliced into 1-inch pieces

4 dried red chiles, such as árbol, left whole

¼ cup Sofregit (page 34) or store-bought sofrito

4 bay leaves

¼ cup Fish Stock (page 35) or store-bought fish stock

Kosher salt and freshly ground black pepper

1 tablespoon chopped fresh curly parsley

1   In a large Dutch oven, heat ¼ cup of the oil over medium-low heat. When the oil is shimmering, add the onions and cook slowly until they are golden brown and almost sticky like onion marmalade, 45 minutes to 1 hour. When they are dark golden brown, transfer the onions to a small bowl.

2   In the same pan, heat the remaining ¼ cup oil over medium heat. When the oil is shimmering, add the garlic and tilt the pan so the cloves have a deep pool of oil to fry in. Fry until the garlic is golden brown, about 2 minutes. Working quickly, return the caramelized onions to the pan and add the octopus. Stir in the chiles, sofregit, and bay leaves and bring the mixture to a simmer, cooking for about 1 minute and stirring frequently. Stir in the stock and cook until the sauce thickens enough to lightly coat the octopus. Season with salt and pepper.

3   Discard the bay leaves and stir in the parsley. Spoon the sauce onto plates and lay the octopus and garlic mixture on top.

POP AMB PATATES

WARM OCTOPUS WITH POTATOES

SERVES 4
AS A FIRST COURSE
OR 6 TO SHARE

In the past, many Catalan households didn't have use for a whole octopus, so housewives would often buy just the fresh tentacles and cook them with a whole potato as a kind of kitchen timer. When the potato was done, so would the tentacles be. Then they would slice the potato and serve it alongside the octopus with a drizzle of olive oil, as done in the recipe here. A pinch of adobo seasoning and a drizzle of pimentón oil make it a bit more special.

1½ pounds fingerling potatoes

Kosher salt

2 tablespoons extra-virgin olive oil

1 teaspoon Adobo Seasoning (page 28), or store-bought adobo plus a generous pinch of pimentón (smoked paprika)

8 tentacles from a 4- to 6-pound octopus, cooked (see opposite) and sliced into ¼- to ½-inch pieces

¼ cup Pimentón Oil (recipe follows)

Pimentón (smoked paprika), for serving (optional)

1   Prepare a large bowl with ice and water. Bring a medium saucepan of water to a boil over high heat. Add the potatoes and a generous pinch of salt. Cook until the potatoes are knife-tender, 15 to 20 minutes. Drain the potatoes and when they are cool enough to handle, slice them into disks about ¼ inch thick (do not remove the skin).

2   In a medium skillet, heat the olive oil over medium heat. When the oil is shimmering, add the potatoes, adobo, and octopus. Cook, tossing gently, until the octopus is heated through, about 5 minutes.

3   Divide the potatoes and octopus among plates, drizzle with pimentón oil, and sprinkle with pimentón, if desired.

OLI DE PEBRE VERNELL

PIMENTÓN OIL

MAKES ABOUT ½ CUP

⅔ cup extra-virgin olive oil

½ medium yellow onion, halved and thinly sliced

2 small garlic cloves, peeled

Kosher salt

1 small bay leaf

1 sprig fresh thyme

1 sprig fresh oregano

3 black peppercorns

⅛ teaspoon pimentón (smoked paprika)

In a large skillet, heat ⅓ cup of the oil over medium-high heat. When the oil is shimmering, add the onion and garlic, season with salt, and reduce the heat to medium-low. Cook slowly until the onion is translucent and the garlic is golden brown, about 15 minutes, stirring frequently. Stir in the bay leaf, thyme, oregano, peppercorns, and remaining ⅓ cup oil. When the onion begins to sizzle, after a minute or two, remove the pan from the heat and stir in the pimentón. Set aside to cool completely, 15 to 30 minutes. Strain the pimentón oil into a mason jar and store at room temperature for up to 4 weeks.

HOW TO COOK OCTOPUS

Look for dark purple octopus with firm flesh and shiny skin. The head should be intact and the octopus should smell of fresh seawater. I don't recommend buying precooked octopus, but frozen is fine. A medium octopus, 3 to 4 pounds, is best because bigger ones will have tougher meat.

To cook a whole octopus, fill a deep stockpot with enough water to have the octopus completely covered when it goes in. Add 1 small peeled and halved onion, 1 small peeled and halved potato, a nice pinch of black peppercorns, and a bay leaf. Bring the water to a boil over high heat. Then use tongs or your hands to hold the octopus by the head and lower it into the pot. After a few seconds, pull the octopus out. Allow the water to return to a boil, then dunk the octopus the same way three more times to gradually introduce it to the boiling water. After the third dip, leave the octopus in the boiling water and let it cook until it is tender, about 1 hour 15 minutes.

Meanwhile, prepare a large bowl of ice and water. When you think the octopus is almost done, check its tenderness: Slice off the thickest tentacle and taste it. If it is cooked properly, it will be tender, but not mushy. If it feels rubbery, return it to the boiling water to cook for another 15 minutes. When the octopus is done, transfer it to the ice bath and let it cool completely, about 15 minutes.

Transfer the cooled octopus to a cutting board and use a sharp knife to cut the head from the tentacles (discard the head). Turn the octopus over and slice the tentacles away from the core of the body. Using a small paring knife, trim the tough membrane away from the thickest part of the tentacles. If the octopus is properly cooked, these tough parts of skin will almost peel back on their own with a knife's suggestion. Once trimmed, the octopus tentacles can be used immediately or wrapped in plastic and refrigerated for up to 3 days.

CEVICHE DE GAMBES AMB POP
SHRIMP, SCALLOP, AND OCTOPUS CEVICHE

Catalans consume an array of seafood and shellfish, and this dish represents that variety, along with more common American flavors such as ketchup and hot sauce. This is bar food at its finest, the kind that Catalans would eat while drinking vermouth on a Sunday with friends (see page 72). It makes the perfect party dish, or you could serve it as a first course alongside a cold beer.

1 tablespoon plus ⅓ cup extra-virgin olive oil, plus more if needed

8 colossal (size U-10) scallops

Kosher salt and freshly ground black pepper

3 bay leaves

8 black peppercorns

8 ounces medium shrimp (21/25 count), peeled, deveined, and cut into 1-inch pieces

3 tablespoons ketchup

2 tablespoons fresh lemon juice

1 teaspoon hot sauce such as El Yucateco Habanero

1 tentacle from a 4- to 6-pound octopus, cooked (see page 147) and sliced into 1-inch pieces

1 small Roma tomato, seeded and finely chopped

¼ cup finely chopped red onion

2 tablespoons finely chopped fresh cilantro

Avocado slices, cilantro leaves, flatbread crackers, and lime wedges, for serving

1   In a large nonstick skillet, heat 1 tablespoon of the oil over high heat. Season the scallops with salt. When the oil is shimmering, add the scallops and sear until golden brown on both sides, about 2 minutes total. Remove the scallops to a plate and refrigerate until cold, at least 15 minutes or up to 1 hour.

2   Meanwhile, prepare a medium bowl of ice and water. Bring a medium saucepan of water to a boil and add the bay leaves and peppercorns. Drop in the shrimp and simmer until bright pink, about 1½ minutes. Using a slotted spoon, transfer the shrimp to the ice bath. Let stand until cold, about 5 minutes, then remove and pat dry.

3   Chill eight small serving bowls. In a large bowl, combine the ketchup, lemon juice, hot sauce, the remaining ⅓ cup olive oil, and a few generous pinches each of salt and pepper.

4   Just before serving, add the shrimp, octopus, tomato, onion, and cilantro to the sauce and toss to coat. The mixture should dress the seafood loosely, which depends on the juiciness of the tomato. Add more oil if necessary. Divide the seafood salad among chilled bowls and top with the scallops, avocado slices, and cilantro leaves. Serve cold with crackers and lime wedges.

TONYINA AMB ESCABETX
TUNA IN ESCABECHE

My mom was known for her sardines in escabeche, a sort of reverse marinade used for preserving cooked fish. You can find tinned fish escabeche throughout Catalonia, but this version is far more refined. Instead of boiled tuna in cans, seared slices of ahi tuna are marinated with the same flavors. I like to let the seared tuna marinate for at least a day so it tastes more intense. Try this tuna in a salad such as Penedès Salad (page 76) or to make the best tuna sandwich you've ever had.

1 pound ahi tuna loin

2 cups extra-virgin olive oil, plus more for searing

Kosher salt

1 medium yellow onion, halved and thinly sliced

¼ cup Roasted Garlic (page 28)

4 bay leaves

1 sprig fresh thyme

1 sprig fresh oregano

½ cup red wine vinegar

2 teaspoons pimentón (smoked paprika)

1   Use a sharp knife to slice the tuna into long rectangles, about 1 × 6 inches. Drizzle the tuna slices with a little bit of oil and sprinkle with salt.

2   Heat a nonstick skillet over high heat. Working with one piece of tuna at a time, quickly sear the tuna all over until the surface of the fish is just opaque and lightly browned, about 15 seconds per side. Remove the pieces to a plate as they are seared.

3   Heat ¼ cup of the oil in the same skillet over medium heat. When the oil is shimmering, add the onion, season with salt, and reduce the heat to medium-low. Cook slowly until the onion is translucent yet keeps its shape, about 15 minutes, stirring often. Stir in the roasted garlic, bay leaves, thyme, oregano, and remaining 1¾ cups oil. When the onions and herbs begin to sizzle, remove the pan from the heat. Stir in the vinegar and pimentón. Pour the mixture into a glass dish that will hold the tuna pieces snugly—an 8-inch square baking dish works well. Set the escabeche mixture aside until it is barely warm to the touch, about 20 minutes.

4   Submerge the tuna in the escabeche mixture and let cool for at least 2 hours or up to 24 hours at room temperature. To serve, remove the fish from the escabeche mixture and slice into ½-inch pieces. Spoon the onion onto plates and top with the fish. Drizzle with some of the escabeche liquid to serve.

RAP A L'ALL CREMAT

MONKFISH AND POTATOES
IN BROWNED GARLIC SAUCE

SERVES 4
AS A FIRST COURSE

Monkfish is considered a humble man's lobster because of its similar texture. When cooked, monkfish doesn't flake like other white fish. If this is your first time working with it, look for the flesh to be cloudy white when it's cooked. This dish comes together quickly, so have the potatoes ready to go.

2 tablespoons pine nuts, toasted

Kosher salt

24 cloves Roasted Garlic (page 28)

⅛ teaspoon pure saffron

4 Roma tomatoes, halved lengthwise

2 tablespoons Garlic Oil (page 28) or extra-virgin olive oil

1 pound monkfish loin, trimmed of belly membrane and silverskin, cut into 8 pieces

2 tablespoons dry white wine

1 cup Fish Stock (page 35) or store-bought fish stock

8 cooked new potatoes (see note), halved

1   Make a *picada* by mashing the pine nuts and a large pinch of salt to a fine paste in a mortar with a pestle. Take your time, as the nuts won't break down easily once you add the rest of the ingredients. Add the garlic and saffron and continue to mash until the garlic is completely broken apart and the picada becomes a thick, golden brown paste resembling peanut butter.

2   Grate the tomatoes on the large holes of box grater, discarding the skins and cores. You should have about 1 cup of pulp.

3   In a large nonstick skillet, heat the oil over high heat. Season the monkfish with salt. When the oil is shimmering, add the monkfish and sear until golden brown on both sides, about 4 minutes total, turning once and shaking the pan occasionally. Stir in the tomato pulp, wine, stock, potatoes, and picada. Increase the heat to high and bring the sauce to a boil. As it comes to a boil, use a spoon to break up the picada and stir it into the sauce around the monkfish. Reduce the heat to medium and simmer until the potatoes are warmed through and the bright golden sauce has thickened to the consistency of heavy cream, about 6 minutes.

4   Serve the monkfish with the potatoes and sauce in shallow bowls.

EL CONSELL: My favorite potatoes to use here are Wrinkly Potatoes (page 95). However, you could also just steam some new potatoes over 1 inch of salted water until tender, about 15 minutes.

ROMESCADA

SEAFOOD STEW WITH ROMESCO

SERVES 4

AS A FIRST COURSE

At the base of *romescada* is one of the most widely used Spanish *picades*, *romesco*, made with roasted almonds, roasted garlic, roasted tomatoes, and the mild ñora chile. This classic quick stew works well as a starter, but you can also double the recipe to create a more substantial main course. I like to leave the heads on the cleaned shrimp because they add a lot of flavor to the dish. However, it helps to peel the shrimp to make them easier to eat in a shallow bowl.

1 tablespoon extra-virgin olive oil

1 tablespoon vegetable oil

8 head-on colossal (U-12 count) shrimp, peeled and deveined, tails left on

4 jumbo sea scallops

12 small clams, such as Manilas

½ cup Romesco (page 32) or store-bought romesco sauce

2 cups Fish Stock (page 35) or store-bought fish stock

1   In a large nonstick skillet, heat the oils over medium-high heat. When the oil is shimmering, add the shrimp and scallops and cook until the shrimp turn bright pink and the scallops are golden brown on both sides, about 4 minutes total, turning once. Remove to a plate and set aside.

2   In the same pan, combine the clams, romesco, and stock. Increase the heat to high, stirring to break up the romesco around the clams as it bubbles, and bring the sauce to a boil. Reduce the heat to medium and simmer until the clams open and the sauce has thickened enough to coat the seafood, about 8 minutes. (Discard any clams that do not open.)

3   Serve all the seafood in bowls with the sauce spooned over the top.

BRANDADA DE BACALLÀ
PUREED SALT COD WITH MASHED POTATOES

Brandada is salty, creamy comfort food served almost like a dip. One of the best parts is the broiled, crunchy top. I like to use individual shallow gratin dishes with a large surface area to help create more of this crust—it's just that good. If you prefer, you could also prepare this recipe family-style in one large baking dish.

1 pound salt cod, desalted (see page 157), drained, and cut into 2-inch pieces

4 bay leaves

10 black peppercorns

¼ cup extra-virgin olive oil

2 medium yellow onions, chopped

Kosher salt

1 pound russet potatoes, peeled and cut into 2-inch pieces

4 tablespoons (½ stick) salted butter

10 garlic cloves, chopped

½ cup heavy cream

2 tablespoons chopped fresh curly parsley

2 tablespoons walnut oil or extra-virgin olive oil, for serving

Flatbread crackers, toasted bread, or crostini, for serving

1 Heat the broiler with a rack in the highest position in the oven.

2 In a medium saucepan, combine the salt cod, bay leaves, and peppercorns and add enough water to cover the ingredients. Bring to a boil over high heat, then reduce the heat to medium and simmer until the cod shreds when pierced with a fork, 8 to 10 minutes. Remove the salt cod to a plate to cool, about 20 minutes. When it is cool enough to handle, finely shred the salt cod with your fingers or a fork.

3   Meanwhile, in a medium saucepan, heat the oil over medium-high heat. When the oil is shimmering, add the onions, season with salt, reduce the heat to medium-low, and cook slowly until they are very soft and light golden brown, about 25 minutes, stirring frequently to prevent burning.

4   While the onions cook, make the mashed potatoes. Put the potatoes in a large pot and add enough cold water to cover by 1 inch. Bring to a boil over high heat and boil until the potatoes are tender, 12 to 15 minutes. Drain the potatoes and return the empty pot to medium heat. Add the butter and when it is melted and foamy, add the garlic. Cook until the garlic is fragrant, about 1 minute, stirring frequently. Stir in the cream and add the drained potatoes. Mash the potatoes with a potato masher or fork until smooth (or use a potato ricer, if you have one). Taste and add salt as needed.

5   Stir the onions, shredded salt cod, and parsley into the mashed potatoes.

6   Transfer the brandada mixture to six to eight individual 4-ounce ramekins or a shallow 1-quart baking dish and smooth the top. If using ramekins, place them on a sheet pan. Broil until the surface is crisp, evenly browned, and lightly charred in spots, 3 to 5 minutes, rotating the dish or pan once or twice for evening browning.

7   Drizzle with walnut oil and serve with crackers, toast, or crostini for dipping and scooping.

BACALLÀ

SALT COD

In Catalonia, *bacallà* is almost worshipped: Shops are set up like holy altars with white, salt-crusted fish perched atop pure white tiles. Salt cod is sold whole, split, with or without skin, and with or without bone. You can buy the tail, broken pieces, the top loin fillet, the cut next to the head, or just the cheeks. It is usually sold in wooden boxes.

Salt cod is one of our oldest preserved foods. Spain, Italy, France, Portugal, and many Caribbean countries used similar methods to preserve cod, prolonging the useful life of the fish. The method has long been associated with frugality and humble food cultures. Consider that a rooster or a pig took resources and time to raise, so meats like chicken and pork were reserved for holiday and celebration meals. Fish, however, were abundant in nearby waters and seen as practically free. Spain has more than three thousand miles of coastline, and the locals were able to harvest mounds and mounds of sea salt very cheaply. To this day, Spanish salt is the primary salt used for preserving fish in Nordic countries. Catalans consider salt cod a staple protein and eat it so regularly that to satisfy the demand, Spain has become the leading importer of salt cod from Iceland (one of the world's largest *bacallà*-producing countries).

The traditional method for salting cod is called "pile salting," in which the fish fillets are stacked between thick layers of coarse salt. The pressure caused by stacking the fish and the salt itself draw moisture from the fish, making it inhabitable to harmful bacteria. Curing methods have changed over the past few decades in favor of speed and consistency, including pickling and brining (or "wet salting"), sometimes in addition to the pile salting method. These shifts in salt cod manufacturing have caused wide variations in the salinity levels of what's on the market, which makes it all the more important to taste the fish after it has been soaked in water to ensure that it is fully "desalted" and enough has been drawn out (see "How to Desalt Salt Cod," below).

With the decline of cod stocks in the world's oceans, be aware that other white fish have become popular substitutes. The term "salt cod" seems to have become generic for salted white fish, particularly pollock. Catalans will insist on the gold standard: a whole fillet of codfish loin roughly 2 inches thick at its thickest point and snow white in color rather than yellow (a yellow color means it has been sitting too long). Of course, the exact cut chosen will vary depending on the market and the dish being prepared. The recipes in this book, such as Salt Cod Fritters (page 56), Penedès Salad (page 76), and Pureed Salt Cod with Mashed Potatoes (page 154), don't require a particular cut of salt cod. Just use the best-quality product you can find. Look for Norwegian salt cod, which is consistently good. Or ask your fishmonger for a good recommendation. You can also make salt cod at home using the recipe at right.

HOW TO DESALT SALT COD

Before using, salt cod must be soaked to desalt it. Place it in a large bowl, add water to cover, and let the fish soak at room temperature for at least 24 hours, changing the water at least once (preferably twice) during that time. After soaking, test the fish by flaking off a small bit and tasting it. It should taste sweet and chewy, and most of its aggressive saltiness should have drained away. Once desalted, the cod can be drained and used as directed in any recipe.

BACALLÀ FET A CASA
HOMEMADE SALT COD

MAKES 2 TO 2½ POUNDS

3 tablespoons kosher salt

1 tablespoon sugar

2 teaspoons pimentón (smoked paprika)

1 large piece (3 pounds) cod loin, about 2 inches thick

About 2 tablespoons extra-virgin olive oil

1   In a small bowl, mix together the salt, sugar, and pimentón. Rub the seasoning all over the fish and place the fish in a shallow perforated pan or on a rack set in a deep baking dish. This will allow moisture to drain away so the fish will cure properly. Wrap the entire pan in plastic wrap and refrigerate for 2 days. Twice a day, flip the fish and gather the excess seasoning from the sides of the dish, scattering it back over the top of the fish each time. It is important for the fish to stay coated in seasoning so it will cure and absorb the flavors.

2   The cod is fully cured when it takes on a pink hue from the pimentón and the flesh feels firm and looks a bit glossy. When cured, rinse the cod under cold water and pat it dry.

3   Place the rinsed cod in a large shallow dish and cover with a thin layer of olive oil. Covered in oil, it will last up to 3 days in the refrigerator. Desalt immediately (see left) or wrap extra salt cod thoroughly in plastic and freeze for up to 3 months.

BACALLÀ FREGIT AMB ALLIOLI DE PERA

SALT COD FRITTERS WITH PEAR AIOLI

SERVES 4
AS A FIRST
COURSE OR TAPA

This recipe is from one of my oldest Spanish chef friends, Adrià Marin, who is the *jefe* of *bacalao* and small bites. He sautés pears in butter with salt and pepper and then purees them. He then stirs some pear puree into a traditional allioli for a fresh take on the sauce. This dish embodies old-school food rising up to meet the new Catalonia. For the best results, use Homemade Salt Cod (page 157) or the highest quality pieces of salt cod loin you can find.

⅓ cup lager, such as Spanish Estrella

1⅓ cups seltzer water

1¼ cups all-purpose flour

2 tablespoons salted butter

1 firm-ripe pear, such as Bartlett or Bosc, stemmed, cored, and cut into wedges

Kosher salt and freshly ground black pepper

½ teaspoon sugar

1 cup Allioli (page 32) or store-bought aioli

About 1 cup vegetable oil, for frying

1 pound salt cod, desalted (see page 157), drained, and cut into 1-ounce squares

1 tablespoon finely sliced fresh chives

1 In a large shallow bowl, whisk together the beer, seltzer, and 1 cup of the flour to form a batter.

2 In a medium saucepan, melt the butter over medium heat. Add the pear and season with a generous pinch each of salt and pepper. Sprinkle the sugar over the top. Cook the pears until they are tender and golden brown in spots, about 7 minutes, shaking the pan occasionally. Transfer the cooked pears to a blender or food processor and pulse until smooth. You should have about ½ cup puree. Add the allioli and pulse to incorporate. Season with salt and pepper to taste.

3 In a medium Dutch oven or other heavy-bottomed pan such as as cast-iron, heat the vegetable oil to 350°F. Place the remaining ¼ cup flour in a medium shallow dish or soup bowl. Working with a few pieces at a time, toss the salt cod in the flour, then drop them into the batter. Working in batches, gently drop the battered salt cod into the oil and fry until evenly crisp and dark golden brown, 2 to 4 minutes, turning it with tongs or a slotted spoon. Transfer the fritters to paper towels to drain.

4 Serve the fritters with the pear allioli and chives. I like to spoon a small amount of pear allioli on the bottom of the plate, then top it with the fritters and another dollop of pear allioli, scattering the chives over the top.

DEL CORRAL
FROM THE CORRAL

The people in the Catalan countryside consist mostly of *pagès* (farmers). Many live far from city centers and raise animals to survive. Furry rabbits may hop and nibble on one side of the farmer's corral while proud roosters and ducks squawk on the other. Sheep and goats often graze in green pastures nearby. Chickens give eggs for daily meals and goats give milk to make cheese, so sacrificing an animal for dinner is not taken lightly and usually reserved for Sunday, a day of reverence for life, when you go to church and the whole family comes together for a big meal in the middle of the afternoon. Many Catalan culinary traditions were developed to celebrate and preserve the delicious meat that you would harvest from your own backyard, including Rabbit Confit (page 167), the mixing of meat and seafood called *mar i muntanya* (see page 172), and several ingenious ways to roast our famous Penedès black-footed rooster (see page 178).

LA FESTA MAJOR

SAINT'S DAY FESTIVAL

Every town in Catalonia has a festival, or *festa major*, to celebrate the city's patron saint. In Vilafranca, we celebrate Saint Fèlix, and our *festa major* is the only one that continued through the decades of Francisco Franco's fascist regime. All the others I know of were required to shut down, but since we were overlooked as "peasants," we were able to operate it illegally. Our *festa major* is a huge event that runs for five days. It signals the beginning and ending of each year even more than the Christian calendar does.

Barcelona has since revived its *festa major*, but towns like Vilafranca are trendier among tourists because our traditions have remained exactly the same for centuries. The dragon costume that appears at the beginning of our festival dates back to the 1400s and symbolizes the potential evil that the town warriors may have to fight off to protect the town and its inhabitants. The head is carved from an ancient olive tree and has survived many decades of fireworks exploding from its gaping maw to mark the festival opening in the center of the city (the cardboard body gets destroyed and replaced every year).

The week's wildest event is called *correfoc*. The name directly translates to "fire-runs"—you have to run away as a live fire heads your way. Despite the danger, it is a point of great pride for spectators to stand in the trails of the hot embers. During *correfoc*, a parade of proud Catalans dress up as devils and spray fireworks into the crowd, as adults and children gamble to see how close they can get without getting burned. After the group of devils finishes its march into a church, the entire downtown area is set ablaze with fireworks.

This group of devils is one of about fifteen different groups featured in the parade, each with medieval origins honoring Saint Fèlix and the former king and queen of Spain. Over the years, the Vilafranca Festa Major has become a bigger and bigger deal, an unstoppable party in the streets with live music at all hours of the night, long pours of vermouth, and huge smiles. The parade begins as soon as the sun rises, and loud drums in the streets wake up anyone who might have nodded off. At this time of year, the city doubles in size, as everyone—including me—returns home to celebrate our heritage.

CONILL AMB BOLETS

RABBIT AND MUSHROOM STEW

SERVES 4
AS A MAIN DISH
OR 6 TO SHARE

One of my oldest friends, Joan Urguell, is from a town about five miles from Vilafranca. His mother, Pepita, taught me this recipe and it has become a favorite of mine. Her version includes snails that she forages along with the mushrooms, but I've omitted them here because fresh snails can be difficult to find. Two other ingredients deepen the flavor of this stew: brandy and chocolate. To improve the flavor even further, chill the stew overnight and enjoy it the next day.

3 tablespoons vegetable oil

1 tablespoon olive oil

1 medium rabbit (2 to 3 pounds), cut into 10 pieces (see page 168)

Kosher salt and freshly ground black pepper

½ ounce dark chocolate, finely chopped

2 slices toasted baguette, crumbled

1 tablespoon finely chopped toasted Marcona almonds

¼ cup brandy

2 tablespoons Sofregit (page 34) or store-bought sofrito

2 bay leaves

1 cinnamon stick

1 sprig fresh thyme, torn into a few pieces

4 ounces small shiitake mushrooms, stems trimmed

1 Mix together the oils, then drizzle the rabbit pieces with 2 tablespoons of the mixed oil and season with salt and pepper. Set aside.

2 Make a *picada* by mashing the chocolate, crumbled toast, and almonds to a fine paste in a mortar with a pestle. Set aside.

3 In a medium Dutch oven, heat the remaining 2 tablespoons mixed oil over medium-high heat. When the oil is shimmering, add the rabbit and sear until golden brown all over, about 4 minutes per side. Stand back and add the brandy, as it may catch on fire. Don't worry—just blow it out and stir up any browned bits from the bottom of the pan.

4 Reduce the heat to low and stir in 1 cup water and the sofregit. Nestle the bay leaves, cinnamon stick, and thyme around the rabbit pieces. Cover and simmer the rabbit over low heat until the flavors blend, about 30 minutes.

5 Gently stir in the mushrooms and chocolate picada around the rabbit. There should be a thin layer of liquid in the bottom of the pan, but if the sauce has simmered away, add water in ¼-cup increments as needed. Cover and cook until the meat shreds easily from the bone, about 20 minutes more.

DEL CORRAL

166

CONILL CONFITAT

RABBIT CONFIT

Confit, or cooking meat in fat and then storing it in the cooled fat, is a timeless European preservation method. It works seamlessly with rabbit, a common meat in Catalan country cooking, and one that benefits from the extra richness. For a crowd, I like to serve the entire dish of rabbit confit with Grilled Bread Salad, alongside Fresh Favas with Peas (page 99) brightened with a splash of brandy.

2 tablespoons plus 2 cups vegetable oil

1 medium rabbit (2 to 3 pounds), cut into 10 pieces (see page 168)

Kosher salt and freshly ground black pepper

6 medium garlic cloves, peeled

1 medium orange, quartered

2 bay leaves

1 sprig fresh rosemary

12 black peppercorns

1 cup extra-virgin olive oil

Grilled Bread Salad (recipe follows), for serving

1 Preheat the oven to 350°F.

2 In a large nonstick skillet, heat 2 tablespoons of the vegetable oil over medium-high heat. Season the rabbit with salt and pepper. When the oil is shimmering, add the rabbit and sear until golden brown all over, about 4 minutes per side. Tuck the meat into a 2-quart baking dish. Scatter the garlic cloves, orange quarters, bay leaves, rosemary, and peppercorns over the rabbit. Pour over the olive oil and remaining 2 cups vegetable oil to cover the meat completely. Be sure the rabbit is completely submerged in oil.

3 Cover with a lid or foil and bake until the meat shreds easily when pierced with a fork, 2½ to 3 hours. Set aside to cool completely to allow the meat to absorb some of the oil and to firm up. You could eat it while warm, but the texture will be soft and the flavor will be less intense than when it is fully "confited," or preserved in fat. Store the rabbit in the oil in the refrigerator for up to 2 days.

4 To serve, reheat the entire dish of confit at 325°F just until warmed through, 15 to 20 minutes. Serve with the bread salad.

(recipe continues)

HOW TO BREAK DOWN A RABBIT

Cutting a rabbit into ten pieces is the best way to serve it to a table of guests. It allows you to cook each piece to perfection—which is not the case when you cook rabbit whole—and gives everyone at the table some variety. You can ask your butcher to do this, but it is easy to do at home.

First remove the back legs by slicing through the hip joint. Then, cut the front legs in the same way. At this point, you'll be left with the loin and ribs, or "saddle." Cut the ribs in half along the backbone, splitting the ribcage in two. Then cut the whole loin crosswise through the backbone into six pieces—all it takes is a little pressure and a sharp knife. Trim the rabbit of any white membrane or excess fat before cooking.

GRILLED BREAD SALAD

SERVES 4

2 tablespoons cava vinegar or champagne vinegar

¼ cup plus 1½ tablespoons extra-virgin olive oil

Kosher salt and freshly ground black pepper

½ loaf day-old Farmer's Bread (page 236) or other round country-style loaf, crust removed and sliced ¼ inch thick

2 green onions, white and light green parts only, thinly sliced

2 garlic cloves, minced

4 cups baby arugula

¼ cup dried currants

1   Pour the vinegar into a large bowl and begin whisking in ¼ cup of the oil drop by drop at first. Continue whisking while adding the oil in a slow, steady stream until all of the oil is incorporated into the vinegar and the mixture thickens, about 1 minute. Season with salt and pepper.

2   Heat a grill or grill pan to medium-high. Brush about half of the vinaigrette on both sides of all the bread slices. Grill the bread until charred all over, 2 to 3 minutes per side. Set aside to cool.

3   Meanwhile, in a small skillet, heat the remaining 1½ tablespoons oil over medium heat. When the oil is shimmering, add the green onions and garlic and sauté until softened but not browned, 2 to 3 minutes. Scrape the mixture into the remaining vinaigrette in the large bowl.

4   Add the arugula to the bowl and toss to coat. Break the cooled bread into large, bite-size pieces, and add it to the bowl along with the currants. Toss to mix, taste, and add salt and pepper if needed. Serve immediately.

POLLASTRE AMB ESCABETX

CHICKEN IN VINAIGRETTE

Back when refrigeration was scarce, chicken was preserved in *escabetx* (escabeche), a sort of pickling liquid that makes it last longer. Soaking the cooked meat in a vinegar-based marinade also infuses it with flavor, which deepens as the days go on. Traditionally, the pickled chicken is served cold with a salad and plenty of crusty bread to soak up the delicious marinade. Make this dish at least a day before you serve it so the chicken has time to absorb the flavorful vinaigrette.

2 tablespoons plus 2 cups extra-virgin olive oil

1 whole chicken (about 3 pounds), cut into 8 pieces

Kosher salt and freshly ground black pepper

1 head garlic, halved horizontally through the equator

2 small carrots, peeled and thinly sliced on the diagonal

½ small yellow onion, halved and thinly sliced

1 leek, halved lengthwise and thinly sliced crosswise into strips

2 cups cava vinegar or champagne vinegar

3 sprigs fresh thyme

3 bay leaves

10 black peppercorns

1   In a large Dutch oven, heat 1 tablespoon of the oil over high heat. Season the chicken generously with salt and pepper. When the oil is shimmering, add about half of the chicken pieces and half of the garlic head, cut-side down. Sear until the chicken skin is evenly golden brown all over, 8 to 10 minutes, shaking the pan and turning the pieces for even cooking. Remove the chicken and garlic to a plate and repeat with another 1 tablespoon oil, the remaining chicken, and the remaining garlic.

2   Add the carrots, onion, and leek to the hot oil in the pan. Cook until the carrots are crisp-tender, about 8 minutes, stirring often. Remove the vegetables from the pan and set aside.

3   Meanwhile, in a medium bowl, whisk together the vinegar, 2 cups water, and the remaining 2 cups oil until combined.

4   Return the cooked chicken and garlic to the pan and pour in the vinegar mixture. Add the thyme, bay leaves, and peppercorns and increase the heat to high. Bring to a boil, then reduce the heat to low, cover, and simmer until the chicken falls apart when pinched with tongs or pierced with a fork, about 1 hour.

5　Remove the pan from the heat and stir in the cooked vegetables. Cover and let stand until barely warm, about 30 minutes. Transfer to the refrigerator and chill for at least 2 hours or up to 2 days. The oil will solidify when chilled, so return the chicken to room temperature before serving.

6　Serve the chicken and vegetables on plates at room temperature, leaving the garlic, thyme sprigs, bay leaves, and peppercorns behind.

EL CONSELL: Ask your butcher to cut your chicken into eight pieces with the legs separated into drumsticks and thighs and each breast cut into two pieces. Or use an equal weight of just thighs and drumsticks if you prefer those cuts.

MAR I MUNTANYA

CATALAN SURF AND TURF

Literally "sea and mountains," *mar i muntanya* is the ultimate symbol of Catalan cuisine, and is quite prevalent in the homes and restaurants of Catalonia today. Its simplest expression is in "surf and turf" dishes such as lobster with rabbit, langoustines with chicken, cuttlefish with meatballs, or squid stuffed with pork sausage. But *mar i muntanya*'s bold flavor combinations are also linked to the region's history and trading patterns among early settlers, in both small-scale bartering between fishermen and farmers and large-scale trading between Spain and other countries in the seaport of Barcelona. It represents the region's history, traditions, and geography in a single dish.

Since the Middle Ages, when *mar i muntanya* originated, Barcelona has been a major hub along the trade routes, connecting ports as far away as Alexandria in Egypt and Amsterdam in the Netherlands. Barcelona continues to be the engine of Spain's economic power today. Over time, the port's many trade relationships have helped to bring a diversity of ingredients such as hazelnuts, pasta, cinnamon, caraway, saffron, and sugar into Catalan cuisine.

Trading also helped Catalans discover different ways to cook with ingredients they already grew in the region. For instance, the ancient Romans liked to include dried fruit in savory preparations, a combination now canonized in the classic Catalan dish of Duck with Prunes and Pine Nuts (page 181).

Perhaps most important, Catalonia's unique geography of a Mediterranean coastline contrasted by ice-capped mountains in the north and fertile river deltas in the south helped to create food traditions that differ from those in the rest of Spain. *Mar i muntanya* embodies this difference. A single Catalan dish can feature foods and flavors from every corner of the region's diverse historical and gastronomical treasure chest.

At its heart, *mar i muntanya* is about resourcefulness. From the sea to the mountains, the Catalan cook creates bold flavor combinations fully expressing the region's culinary diversity, incorporating ingredients and cooking methods gained through bartering and preserving, foraging and fishing, or raising and harvesting the region's incredible local foods.

POLLASTRE AMB GAMBES

CHICKEN WITH SHRIMP

This recipe is a time-honored example of *mar i muntanya*, the Catalan version of surf and turf celebrating all of our regions in a single dish. It also showcases a nut-based *picada*, which tastes best when pounded just before being stirred into the dish. Traditionally, this dish is shared at the table after everyone polishes off paella. Try it following a course of Seafood Paella (page 111) or Rice with Seafood (page 126).

1 tablespoon extra-virgin olive oil

1 tablespoon vegetable oil

2 large boneless, skin-on chicken breast halves (about 2 pounds total)

Kosher salt and freshly ground black pepper

8 shell-on large shrimp (16/20 count)

1 leek, halved lengthwise and sliced into ¼-inch pieces

½ small yellow onion, halved and thinly sliced

½ cup Sofregit (page 34) or store-bought sofrito

About 2 cups Chicken Stock (page 35) or store-bought chicken stock

2 bay leaves

1 sprig fresh thyme

1 sprig fresh oregano

2 tablespoons almonds, toasted

2 tablespoons skinless hazelnuts, toasted

1 small garlic clove, roughly chopped

2 tablespoons cream sherry, such as sweetened Oloroso

1   Mix the oils together. In a large nonstick skillet, heat 1 tablespoon of the mixed oil over medium-high heat. Season the chicken with salt and pepper. When the oil is shimmering, add the chicken skin-side down, and sear until the skin shrinks and is golden and crisp, about 5 minutes. Turn the meat and cook until about halfway cooked, another 4 to 5 minutes. While the chicken cooks, sear the shrimp alongside it, cooking until the flesh under their shells turns pink on both sides, about 3 minutes total. Remove the chicken and shrimp to a plate.

2   Reduce the heat under the skillet to medium and add the remaining 1 tablespoon mixed oil. When the oil is shimmering, stir in the leek and onion, cover, and cook until tender, 6 to 8 minutes, stirring occasionally. Uncover and stir in the sofregit and 1 cup of stock, scraping up any browned bits from the bottom of the pan as the mixture simmers. Return the chicken to the pan and add enough additional stock to come about three-fourths of the way up the chicken. Add the bay leaves, thyme, and oregano and bring to a simmer. Reduce the heat to low, cover, and braise gently until the chicken is just shy of cooked through, 10 to 15 minutes, turning once.

3   While the chicken braises, make a picada by mashing the nuts and garlic to a fine paste in a mortar with a pestle. Stir in the sherry.

4   Remove the chicken to a plate, and strain the sauce through a fine-mesh strainer. Return the sauce to the skillet along with the chicken, shrimp, and picada. Simmer quickly until the chicken is cooked through but still tender inside, about 5 minutes. Slice each chicken breast in half, place the chicken and shrimp on plates, then spoon the sauce over the top.

EL CONSELL: If you have a little grappa in your bar stash, stir it in along with the sherry to add another dimension of flavor.

POLLASTRE ROSTIT A LA GREIXONERA

ROASTED CHICKEN IN A DUTCH OVEN

SERVES 4 TO 6
AS A MAIN DISH

Fermí Puig is one of the most highly respected chefs cooking traditional Catalan food in Catalonia today. He was the original chef at the restaurant that chef Ferran Adrià eventually made famous as El Bulli, and I consider Fermí to be the godfather of classic Catalan cuisine. The last time I visited Fermí at his namesake restaurant, he was kind enough to cook his traditional roast chicken for me. He gave me several ideas for roasting our region's revered Penedès black-footed rooster, and this dish is my tip of the hat to him to return the favor of his hospitality.

1 large free-range rooster or stewing chicken (about 4 pounds)
Kosher salt and freshly ground black pepper
½ cup lard
2 sprigs fresh oregano
1 cinnamon stick
2 medium yellow onions, thinly sliced
1½ pounds russet potatoes, peeled and cut into 1-inch cubes
½ cup extra-virgin olive oil
12 garlic cloves, peeled
2 teaspoons brandy

1 Preheat the oven to 375°F.

2 Place the bird in a large bowl and season it generously with 1½ teaspoons salt and 1 teaspoon pepper inside and out. Use your hands to coat the bird all over with ¼ cup of the lard, including inside the cavity. Work your fingers under the skin of each breast to loosen it and tuck a sprig of oregano underneath each. Place the cinnamon stick inside the bird near the neck.

3 Place the onions in a large bowl and season generously with salt and pepper, tossing to coat and separating the onions into rings. Toss the potatoes in a separate large bowl with generous pinches each of salt and pepper.

4 In a medium Dutch oven, heat the remaining ¼ cup lard and the olive oil over medium heat, swirling the pan until the lard melts and the fats combine. Add the potatoes, onions, and garlic and cook until the vegetables begin to sizzle, 2 to 3 minutes. Place the bird on top of the vegetables and drizzle it with the brandy.

5 Cover and transfer the pan to the oven. Roast until the bird is halfway cooked, about 25 minutes. Increase the oven temperature to 475°F and roast until the liquid in the pan reduces in volume by about one-third, about 30 minutes more. Uncover and continue roasting the chicken until the skin is crisp and browned and the juices run clear when pierced, 35 to 45 minutes more. Carefully remove the chicken from the pan and transfer it to a cutting board. Leave the oven on.

6 Let the chicken rest for 10 to 15 minutes, then carve it into 8 serving pieces, discarding the cinnamon stick and oregano sprigs. If any of the chicken pieces are undercooked, return those pieces to the pan and roast until cooked through.

7 Strain the vegetables from the broth and serve them with the chicken.

FIRA DEL GALL

THE FESTIVAL OF THE PENEDÈS
BLACK-FOOTED ROOSTER

At the end of December, usually right before Christmas, my hometown of Vilafranca celebrates the local black-footed rooster in a festival called Fira del Gall. It is a celebration of culinary and agricultural history with deep roots in my home region of Penedès. Every year a new figurine is made to commemorate the rooster, and the figurine remains displayed in local store windows throughout the year. The Fira del Gall is a unique food festival, and I've never seen anything like it anywhere.

The event began as a medieval poultry market, which featured our native rooster. Over time, the striking appearance and fine meat of this bird became so famous that the Penedès black-footed rooster came to enjoy PGI-status (Protected Geographical Indication) to ensure its proper origin and breeding. It has now become nothing short of a national treasure. Local farmers tend to these exalted birds by feeding them a diet of roasted grape seeds and allowing them to roam freely in their pastures. The Penedès black-footed rooster takes almost three times as long—and far more resources— to foster to maturity than a standard chicken. But the investment of time and energy is made out of passion and pride as well as respect for tradition and great flavor.

At the festival, the main square in Vila-franca, called the *rambles*, transforms into rows of booths hosted by local restaurants offering bites of food in honor of the famed rooster. Other booths are stacked with cages containing the roosters, proudly displaying their shiny black plumes, dark gray feet, and crimson combs. Anyone can purchase one of these prized roosters while it is still alive and take it to a designated trailer where their chosen bird is butchered to order. The customer brings home their fresh poultry in time for Christmas as a centerpiece of the holiday festivities.

Traditionally, there are three different ways of cooking this fine rooster: braised, roasted, or a hybrid of roast and confit. Each family does it its own way, choosing to cook the bird whole or in pieces, selecting different fats, and adjusting the heat high or low. Most Catalan mothers and grandmothers prefer to slowly cook the rooster in a 1:1 mixture of lard and olive oil, confiting it—perhaps with a stick of cinnamon. The cooked rooster meat is very lean and firm, and slow-cooking with plenty of fat makes it irresistibly succulent. Try the recipe for Roasted Chicken in a Dutch Oven (page 176) to get a taste. If you can get a hold of a Penedès rooster, you could also use it in the recipe for Duck with Prunes and Pine Nuts (page 181), another classic presentation of this magnificent bird.

ÀNEC A LA CATALANA
DUCK WITH PRUNES AND PINE NUTS

Catalan celebration dishes often feature the flavor combination of pine nuts and dried fruit. Pine nuts are a luxury ingredient for humble households, so this dish is usually saved for holidays and other occasions when the whole family comes over for dinner. I like to start off such meals with a lighter course, such as Seafood Stew with Romesco (page 152). That opens the palate for the rich and savory flavors here, which are perfectly complemented by a bold red wine such as *garnatxa* from Priorat.

12 garlic cloves, peeled

2 teaspoons kosher salt

2 teaspoons ground cinnamon

2 tablespoons pimentón (smoked paprika)

1 tablespoon ground cumin

2 tablespoons chopped fresh curly parsley

¼ cup extra-virgin olive oil

6 duck legs (about 2¼ pounds)

2 large carrots, peeled and chopped

2 yellow onions, halved and thinly sliced

5 Roma tomatoes, halved lengthwise

4 to 5 sprigs fresh thyme

2 cups cream sherry, such as sweetened Oloroso

4 cups Chicken Stock (page 35) or store-bought chicken stock

8 pitted dried prunes, halved lengthwise

1 tablespoon pine nuts, toasted

1   Mince 2 of the garlic cloves and place in a small bowl. Stir in 1 teaspoon of the salt, the cinnamon, pimentón, cumin, parsley, and oil until combined. Rub the duck all over with the spice paste. Cover with plastic wrap and marinate in the refrigerator overnight.

2   Preheat the oven to 350°F.

3   In a roasting pan, toss together the carrots, onions, tomatoes, thyme, and remaining 10 garlic cloves and 1 teaspoon of salt. Place the seasoned duck legs over the vegetables. Pour in the sherry and 2 cups water. Bring to a boil over medium-high heat, then cover the pan with foil and transfer to the oven. Roast until the meat falls off the bones when pierced with a knife, 2½ to 3 hours. Remove the duck to a sheet pan and let rest at room temperature until it is barely warm, about 1 hour.

4   Meanwhile, strain the contents of the roasting pan through a fine-mesh strainer into a medium bowl, using a pestle or wooden spoon to press the cooked vegetables, squeezing out all of their liquid (discard the solids).

(recipe continues)

Let the liquid cool until warm, about 20 minutes, then cover and refrigerate until cold, at least 1 hour. Use a spoon to skim off and discard the fat that rises to the surface, leaving the pure liquid beneath.

5   Heat the broiler with a rack in the highest position in the oven.

6   In a medium saucepan, combine the skimmed cooking liquid and stock and bring to a simmer over medium heat. Simmer until the sauce reduces in volume by a little less than half, and thickens enough to coat the back of a spoon, about 20 minutes. Add the prunes halfway through cooking.

7   Meanwhile, broil the duck on the sheet pan until crispy and browned, 4 to 5 minutes, rotating the pan halfway through for even browning.

8   Plate the duck legs with the prunes and spoon the sauce over the meat. Sprinkle with the toasted pine nuts.

GUATLLA A L'ALLET
QUAIL IN BROWNED GARLIC SAUCE

Cooking meat *a l'allet* is an old tradition in Catalonia because it's inexpensive and easy to make. Hunted game birds, rabbit, and rooster are all cooked this way. I now live in Texas, where the local game bird is quail, and this classic preparation works perfectly. I deepen the flavor by marinating the birds overnight.

4 semi-boneless quail (4 to 5 ounces each)
Kosher salt and freshly ground black pepper
6 tablespoons extra-virgin olive oil
10 small garlic cloves, minced
¾ cup dry white wine
2 cups Chicken Stock (page 35) or store-bought chicken stock
2 ounces frisée lettuce, trimmed
1 teaspoon cava vinegar or champagne vinegar
Chopped fresh curly parsley, for serving

1   Place the quail in a small baking dish and rub them all over with salt, pepper, and 2 tablespoons of the olive oil. Cover tightly with plastic wrap and marinate overnight in the refrigerator.

2   Preheat the oven to 475°F.

3   In a large nonstick skillet, heat 3 tablespoons of the oil over medium-high heat. When the oil is shimmering, add the quail breast-side down and cook, without moving, until browned across the breast, 3 to 4 minutes total. Transfer the quail to a sheet pan, breast-side up, reserving the skillet with the caramelized bits.

4   Roast the quail until the juices run clear, 5 to 8 minutes.

5   Meanwhile, return the reserved skillet to medium heat. Add the garlic and cook until golden brown, about 1 minute, stirring often. Add the wine and increase the heat to high, stirring to scrape any browned bits from the bottom of the pan. Cook until the wine is mostly evaporated, about 3 minutes. Add the stock and cook until the liquid reduces in volume, thickens, and turns deep golden brown, about 10 minutes.

6   Just before serving, toss the frisée with the vinegar and the remaining 1 tablespoon oil in a medium bowl. Season with salt and pepper.

7   Divide the salad among four plates. Top each pile of salad with a quail, then spoon the pan sauce on top. Garnish with some fresh parsley.

PX VINEGAR

One of my favorite flavors on grilled lamb chops is Pedro Ximénez (PX) vinegar, made from Spanish sherry grapes that have been dried in the sun to intensify their flavor. The good stuff is usually aged for about ten years. At that point, this thick, black vinegar develops notes of cherry, tobacco, and raisins. When I drizzle PX vinegar on marinated and grilled lamb chops, it tastes like home. Look for this vinegar online or at Spanish import stores. It should taste sweet and tangy at the same time. If you can't find PX vinegar, use the best aged balsamic you can find.

COSTELLES DE XAI A LA BRASA

GRILLED LAMB CHOPS WITH PEDRO XIMÉNEZ VINEGAR

SERVES 2 AS A MAIN DISH OR 4 TO SHARE

During a recent visit back home, a friend and local shepherd, Salvador Queraltó, brought me to his corral to see his herd. We took a walk I will never forget. Salvador is known for raising the best meat in town, and I was lucky enough to learn his secret: He grazes his sheep in the vineyards nearby as a sustainable way to prune the grapevines. The animals enjoy the change in their diet and scenery, and the winemakers don't have to prune their vines as often. It is a beautiful harmony resulting in the best lamb I have ever tasted. Of course, Salvador's lamb is impossible to get outside of Penedès, so I use New Zealand lamb chops whenever I make this dish away from home.

1 tablespoon extra-virgin olive oil

1 sprig fresh rosemary, leaves stripped and finely chopped

1 garlic clove, chopped

Kosher salt and freshly ground black pepper

4 lamb rib chops (about 1 pound), frenched

1 to 2 teaspoons PX vinegar (see opposite) or aged balsamic vinegar

Flaky sea salt, for serving

1   In a small bowl, stir together the oil, rosemary, garlic, and a generous pinch each of salt and pepper. Rub the mixture all over the lamb chops and transfer them to a small baking dish. Press parchment onto the surface of the lamb and wrap the entire dish in plastic to seal. (The parchment helps prevent the lamb from oxidizing or reacting to light.) Refrigerate for at least 1 hour or overnight. Let the chops rest at room temperature for 30 minutes before grilling.

2   Heat the grill or grill pan to medium-high. Add the chops and cook to medium-rare, 6 to 8 minutes total, rotating and flipping them often for even browning. Transfer to plates, and sprinkle with a dash of vinegar and flaky salt before serving.

EL CONSELL: It may be less expensive to buy a rack of lamb and french it yourself. Just cut the rack into individual rib chops, then trim the excess fat and membranes from the ribs. The chops will then resemble lollipops.

ESCUDELLA I CARN D'OLLA

CATALAN MEAT AND VEGETABLE STEW

SERVES 8

AS A COMBINATION
FIRST COURSE AND
MAIN DISH

This Catalan one-pot meal is traditionally served at Christmas. A variety of meats, including meatballs, simmer together slowly in their own broth along with vegetables, chickpeas, and pasta, creating a filling feast for a large family. The finished dish is enjoyed as several different courses: The broth and pasta are ladled into soup bowls as a first course, followed by the meats served on a platter alongside the vegetables and chickpeas, all of which is drizzled with a extra-virgin olive oil for added richness. Vary the meats to suit your taste. This stew is a great place to use up odds and ends, and your butcher will likely be more than willing to give you some neck and shank bones.

PILOTES (MEATBALLS)

2 slices country bread, crusts removed

½ cup whole milk

2 large eggs, beaten

2 tablespoons chopped fresh curly parsley

2 tablespoons pine nuts, toasted

1 garlic clove, roughly chopped

½ teaspoon ground cinnamon

Kosher salt and freshly ground black pepper

8 ounces fennel pork sausage (such as Italian sweet sausage), casings removed, or Homemade Spicy Loose Catalan Sausage (page 203)

8 ounces ground veal

STEW

1 bone from a cured ham, such as Serrano, or a fresh ham hock (about 1 pound)

1 pound mixed veal and pork bones, such as neck and shank, rinsed well

4 ounces cured ham, such as Serrano

2 pounds mixed meats, such as 1 whole chicken leg (thigh and drumstick) and oxtail

1 cup dried chickpeas, soaked overnight and drained

1 celery rib, cut into large pieces

1 leek, cut into large pieces

2 pounds root vegetables, such as turnips, parsnips, and carrots, peeled and cut into large pieces

1 medium yellow onion, peeled and quartered

1 pound russet potatoes, peeled and quartered

½ small head green cabbage (about 8 ounces), quartered

1 link (4 ounces) morcilla or other blood sausage

8 ounces medium shell pasta

Extra-virgin olive oil, for serving

1   Prepare the *pilotes*: In a medium bowl, combine the bread and milk and let stand until the bread has lost its firm texture, at least 30 minutes. Stir in the eggs, parsley, pine nuts, garlic, cinnamon, 2 teaspoons salt, and 1 teaspoon pepper. Add the sausage and ground veal and mix well with your hands. Portion the meat mixture into thirty 2-inch balls, rounding them between your palms.

2   Make the stew: Fill a large pot with 1 gallon water and add the ham bone, veal and pork bones, cured ham, and mixed meats. Bring to a boil over high heat. As the water comes to a boil, use a large spoon to skim off any froth that floats to the top.

3   Add the chickpeas, reduce the heat to medium, and simmer slowly until the chickpeas begin to soften, about 30 minutes. Skim the froth again. Add the celery, leek, root vegetables, and onion. Increase the heat to high and return to a boil. Skim the froth again. (The more you skim the froth as the stew cooks, the clearer the broth will be when it's finished.) Cook until the vegetables are tender when pierced with a fork, about 30 minutes. Add the potatoes, cabbage, morcilla, and meatballs and cook until tender, about 15 minutes, skimming occasionally.

4   Use a slotted spoon to remove the meat, vegetables, and chickpeas from the broth and transfer to a platter. Cover with foil to keep warm. Return the broth to a simmer and add the pasta. Cook to al dente, 8 to 10 minutes.

5   To serve, spoon the broth and pasta into serving bowls. Slice the morcilla and arrange among the meats, meatballs, vegetables, and cooked chickpeas on the platter. Drizzle generously with olive oil.

CANELONS
BRISKET CANELONES

During their own *festes majors*, all towns in Catalonia feature *canelons*. The iconic feast dish, sheets of egg-based pasta rolled into tubes, stuffed with a variety of roasted meats, and topped with a rich, creamy sauce and grated cheese, always symbolizes opulence and festivity. Canelons take effort to make, so it helps to start them a day ahead and enlist family members to help. The twist I add is to use brisket—a choice inspired by my adopted town of Austin, Texas, and its love for the barbecued variety.

BRISKET AND MUSHROOM FILLING

Kosher salt and freshly ground black pepper

1 tablespoon ground cumin

1 tablespoon mild chili powder

1½ teaspoons light brown sugar

1½ teaspoons granulated sugar

1 beef brisket (4 pounds), fat trimmed to ⅛-inch thickness

1 tablespoon extra-virgin olive oil

1 tablespoon vegetable oil

1 garlic clove, finely chopped

2 tablespoons chopped fresh curly parsley

8 ounces sliced mixed fresh mushrooms, such as oyster, portobello, and shiitake

1 cup Sofregit (page 34) or store-bought sofrito

BÉCHAMEL SAUCE

4 tablespoons (½ stick) salted butter

1 small yellow onion, finely chopped

¼ cup all-purpose flour

2 cups whole milk

½ teaspoon freshly grated nutmeg

Kosher salt

ASSEMBLY

Butter for the baking dish

18 Spanish canelons pasta sheets (see note)

4 ounces Manchego cheese, grated

1   Make the brisket: In a small bowl or cup, combine 1 tablespoon salt, 1½ teaspoons pepper, the cumin, chili powder, and both sugars. Rub the spice mixture all over the brisket on a large sheet pan. Cover with plastic and marinate in the refrigerator for at least 5 hours or up to overnight.

2   Preheat the oven to 300°F.

3   Heat a large griddle or skillet over high heat. When the pan is smoking, add the brisket and sear until browned on all sides, about 15 minutes total, turning a few times. Transfer the brisket fat-side down to a large, shallow baking dish and wrap the dish tightly in a double layer of foil. Roast until the brisket shreds easily when pierced with a fork, about 6 hours.

4   Transfer the brisket to a large bowl and set aside to cool. When cool enough to handle, about 30 minutes, shred the meat into bite-size pieces.

5   While the brisket cools, make the mushrooms: In a large nonstick skillet, heat the oils over medium-high heat. When the oil is shimmering, add the garlic and parsley and cook until the garlic is fragrant, about 1 minute, stirring frequently. Add the mushrooms and cook until they release their liquid and become lightly browned, about 10 minutes, stirring often. Remove the pan from the heat and let the mixture cool until just warm, about 15 minutes.

6   Make the filling: Transfer the shredded brisket and mushrooms to a food processor and pulse until chopped (see note). Add the sofregit and pulse again until the filling is combined and finely chopped but not pureed. You can refrigerate the filling in an airtight container for up to 2 days.

7   Make the béchamel sauce: In a medium saucepan, melt the butter over medium heat. When the butter is foamy, add the onion and reduce the heat to medium-low. Cook slowly until the onion is translucent, about 15 minutes, stirring often. Stir the flour into the onion and cook until it bubbles and looks foamy, about 5 minutes. Add the milk and bring to a simmer, whisking almost constantly until the sauce thickens, 8 to 10 minutes. Stir in the nutmeg and ½ tablespoon salt.

8   Assemble the dish: Preheat the oven to 450°F. Butter a 13 × 9-inch baking dish.

9   Bring a large pot of salted water to a boil. Add the pasta and cook to al dente, about 6 minutes. Drain and pat dry between clean kitchen towels.

10 Lay out the cooked pasta sheets on a clean work surface and add about ¼ cup filling in a line along one of the short sides. Fold the pasta over the filling, and continue to roll up and enclose. Arrange the canelons seam-side down in the prepared baking dish. Pour the béchamel over the canelons, then scatter on the Manchego. Bake the canelons until browned and bubbling, about 20 minutes. Let cool slightly and serve warm.

EL CONSELL: I use Gallo brand canelons pasta sheets. If you can't find them, use 3 fresh lasagna sheets and cut them into 5 × 6-inch rectangles.

For the best texture in the filling, pass the shredded brisket and mushrooms through the coarse holes of a meat grinder before mixing in the sofregit.

ESTOFAT DE CUA DE BOU
OXTAIL IN RED WINE SAUCE

Growing up in Vilafranca, I always saw oxtails sitting at the meat market. They are an inexpensive cut of beef no one seemed to know what to do with. While working at Zuni Café in San Francisco, I saw how slow-cooking transformed oxtails into an incredibly luscious plate of food. We would leave them near the cinders of the wood-burning oven to slowly braise overnight—the meat tasted incredible the next day. Here, the braising method is similar but done in a home oven for a shorter period of time. I like to season the beef and let the flavors deepen overnight, so start this dish the day before you plan to cook it. I use the same red wine here that I use for sangria—nothing fancy. As long as it is good and dry, it will work. The best accompaniment to this dish is a mound of creamy mashed potatoes, made with a few cloves of mashed Roasted Garlic (page 28), into which you can spoon the braised oxtail and its gravy.

5 pounds oxtail, patted dry

Kosher salt and freshly ground black pepper

1 tablespoon extra-virgin olive oil

1 tablespoon vegetable oil

1 cup dry red wine

1 cup Sofregit (page 34) or store-bought sofrito

2 cups Beef Stock (page 35) or store-bought beef stock

1 small carrot, cut into 2-inch pieces on the diagonal

1 small yellow onion, cut into 1-inch pieces

2 celery ribs, cut into 2-inch pieces

4 sprigs fresh thyme

6 black peppercorns

1 bay leaf

1 Generously season the oxtails all over with salt and pepper. Let sit in the refrigerator for at least 4 hours or overnight.

2 Preheat the oven to 350°F.

3 Remove the beef from the refrigerator and season it with a little more salt and pepper. In a large Dutch oven, heat the oils over high heat. When the oil is shimmering, add the oxtails in batches and sear until a thick brown crust forms, about 8 minutes per side. A good dark sear is crucial here, so don't rush it. Remove to a roasting pan as the pieces are done.

4   Add the wine, sofregit, and stock to the Dutch oven, scraping up any browned bits from the bottom of the pan. Pour the mixture into the roasting pan with the oxtail. Scatter the carrot, onion, celery, thyme, peppercorns, and bay leaf around the oxtails in the pan, submerging the ingredients in the liquid.

5   Cover the pan with foil and roast until the beef falls apart when squeezed with tongs, 5 to 6 hours. Remove the oxtails to a cutting board and shred the meat from the bones. Set the meat aside in a medium saucepan and cover to keep warm.

6   Strain the roasting pan contents through a fine-mesh strainer into a medium bowl, using a pestle or wooden spoon to press the cooked vegetables, squeezing out all their liquid (discard the solids). Let the liquid cool until just warm, about 20 minutes, then cover and refrigerate until cold, at least 1 hour. Use a spoon to skim the fat that has risen to the surface, leaving the pure liquid beneath.

7   Stir the skimmed cooking liquid into the shredded meat in the saucepan and reheat gently over medium-low, about 5 minutes. Serve warm.

"CHORIBURGER"

BEEF-CHORIZO HAMBURGER
WITH MANCHEGO

SERVES 4

Americans enjoy burgers as sandwiches while Catalans prefer chorizo sandwiches. I thought: Why not combine the two? I like to use fresh Spanish chorizo here, called *masa*. It's the loose pork mixture before it is stuffed into casings and cured. But fresh Mexican chorizo, which is much easier to come by, will work well. Or make your own Homemade Spicy Loose Catalan Sausage (page 203). Serve these burgers with a cold beer and some potatoes, such as Fried Potatoes with Spicy Tomato Sauce and Allioli (page 41) or roasted russet potato wedges sprinkled with Adobo Seasoning (page 28).

1 pound fresh chorizo, casings removed

1 pound lean ground beef

Kosher salt and freshly ground black pepper

4 ounces Manchego cheese, coarsely grated

4 ciabatta hamburger rolls, split and toasted

Allioli (page 32) or store-bought aioli, for serving

Tomato slices and romaine leaves, for serving

Pickled Red Onions (page 212), for serving

1   Heat a grill or grill pan to medium-high.

2   In a large bowl, gently mix together the chorizo and beef with your hands. Divide the meat into 4 equal portions and shape gently into patties about 1 inch thick. Season all over with salt and pepper.

3   Grill the burgers to medium-rare, 6 to 8 minutes total, flipping once. During the last 2 minutes of cooking, pile the cheese on the burgers, put down the grill lid or cover with a large lid or baking pan, and cook until the cheese melts.

4   Spread each toasted bun with allioli. Add the burgers and top with the tomato slices, lettuce, and pickled onions.

FROM THE CORRAL

197

EL NOSTRE AMIC, EL PORC
OUR FRIEND, THE PIG

Growing up in Vilafranca, I would ride my bicycle through nearby towns and see pigs on every farmstead. Pork is revered for its flavor and versatility throughout Catalonia. Pigs are relatively easy to raise, the meat cures well, and we appreciate every cut. The sacrifice of the animal, called the *matança*, is a traditional community affair resulting in choice cuts and several different sausages for the participants. There's an old saying in Catalan: *El porc, sigui xic o sigui gros, vuit llonganisses duu al cos* (The body of a pig, whether big or small, can make eight sausages in all). Out of respect for the animal, Catalans tend to prepare pork simply, although we do use it liberally in our cooking.

XORIÇO AMB CIGRONS
GRILLED CHORIZO AND CHICKPEAS

Xoriço (chorizo) is the most well-known pork sausage in Catalonia. Some *cansaladers* (meat curers) make it fresh and some cure it; some make it long and thin; some make it short and thick. Look for links of fresh Spanish chorizo for this dish, or use links of fresh Mexican chorizo. When I was a kid, chorizo was one of my favorite pork sausages, and once a week my mom would cook it with chickpeas, garlic, and parsley, as here. To add some crunch and freshness, I like to serve this dish with pickled onions and chimichurri.

CHIMICHURRI

2 tablespoons fresh thyme leaves

2 tablespoons fresh oregano leaves

¼ cup fresh curly parsley leaves

2 garlic cloves, roughly chopped

Kosher salt

¼ teaspoon pimentón (smoked paprika)

¼ cup extra-virgin olive oil

1 tablespoon red wine vinegar

1 small bay leaf

1 fresh árbol chile or cayenne chile, halved lengthwise

CHORIZO AND CHICKPEAS

4 links (3 ounces each) fresh Spanish chorizo

1 tablespoon extra-virgin olive oil

4 garlic cloves, finely chopped

3 cups cooked or canned chickpeas, drained and rinsed

1 cup Vegetable Stock (page 35) or store-bought vegetable stock

½ cup Pickled Red Onions (page 212), for serving

1   Make the chimichurri: Mash the thyme, oregano, parsley, garlic, and a generous pinch of salt in a mortar with a pestle until it becomes a fine paste. Scrape the mixture into a medium bowl and stir in the pimentón. Whisk in the oil, vinegar, bay leaf, and chile. Cover the bowl with plastic wrap and set aside in a warm place for the flavors to meld, at least 2 hours. Discard the bay leaf and chile before using.

2   Make the chorizo and chickpeas: Heat a grill or grill pan to medium-high. Add the sausages and cook until plump and charred in spots but still juicy inside, about 8 minutes, turning frequently. Remove to a plate and cover with foil to keep warm.

3   Meanwhile, in a large skillet, heat the oil over medium-high heat. When the oil is shimmering, add the garlic and cook until light golden brown, about 1 minute, stirring frequently. Add the chickpeas and stock and simmer until the liquid mostly evaporates, about 5 minutes, shaking the pan occasionally.

4   To serve, divide the chickpeas among four plates and top with the sausages. Spoon the chimichurri on top and scatter the pickled onions around.

EL CONSELL: If you're in a time crunch, you could buy good-quality chimichurri in place of the one made here. Just add a pinch of pimentón to give it a smoky aroma.

You can also make this dish in a cast-iron pan on the stovetop. Just heat the pan over medium-high heat, add a drizzle of oil, and sear the sausages in the hot oil. The skins will split and the sausage will be done after 8 to 10 minutes.

CATALAN XARCUTERIA

MEAT MARKETS IN CATALONIA

The most important food shops in Catalonia are the bakeries, the fish markets, and the *xarcuteria* (pork stores). The town of Vic, an hour north of Barcelona, is home to some of Catalonia's most famous xarcuteria, but in every Catalan town, the sausage maker is considered a pillar of the local food industry.

When you step into a Catalan xarcuteria, rich aromas of warm lard and salted cured hams engulf your senses. At least seventeen distinct varieties of sausage are unique to Catalonia. *Botifarra* has the deepest roots in the region. Ancient recipes led to several modern forms of botifarra, from raw and cured varieties to black and white types and those including egg, truffles, tripe, rice, and blood.

Catalans love pork, and I encourage you to try as many of this region's distinctive and delicious sausages as you can. Several can be found at Spanish purveyors online. Better yet, go to Catalonia! Here is a glimpse of what you will see in a typical xarcuteria, courtesy of my good friend and third-generation sausage-maker, Salvador Valls, who runs his family's artisanal xarcuteria in Vilafranca.

BOTIFARRA BLANCA: A pale white sausage made from a blend of lean and fatty cuts of pork. The best versions are light tasting, very delicate in texture, and fragrant like French *boudin blanc*. A point of pride for Salvador is that his botifarra contains only salt and pepper, no other spices, upholding the tradition of true *blanca* sausage. For a simple homemade botifarra, see Homemade Spicy Loose Catalan Sausage, opposite.

BOTIFARRA NEGRA: Catalonia's version of *morcilla* sausage, *botifarra negra* is a blood sausage often containing rice or bread as a binder.

If the sausage is particularly thick and dense, it may be called *bisbe*. Botifarra negra frequently shows up in *escudella i carn d'olla* (Catalan Meat and Vegetable Stew, page 188) as part of a Catalan Christmas feast. Any home-style restaurant in a rural stretch of Catalonia would serve this sausage for breakfast with Catalan Tomato Bread (page 38) and possibly a fried egg.

FUET, ESPETEC, AND SECALLONA: These are all varieties of Catalan dry-cured *llonganissa*. Since childhood, my favorite sausage of this type is *fuet*, which translates to "whip," as an indicator of its slim shape. Similar to Spanish *longaniza fina*, this long and thin sausage is flecked with fat and blended with salt, pepper, and occasionally anise. It has a chalky white coating on the casing and slices smoothly into little coins. It's perfect for a cheese plate.

SOBRASSADA: Originally from the Balearic Islands, *sobrassada* has become so beloved by Catalans that we treat it as our own. This cured sausage has a soft texture and is heavily spiced with pimentón and occasionally cayenne. Enjoy it in a sandwich such as Grilled Manchego and Sausage Sandwich (page 75).

XORIÇO: Spanish chorizo is very different from the Mexican variety. Mexican chorizo is almost always sold raw in the meat case, while the Spanish variety is often cured or smoked and sold in the deli. Mexican chorizo is also very fatty and usually contains chiles and vinegar, while Spanish chorizo is leaner and not usually very spicy. Both have paprika to thank for their reddish hue. Cured Spanish chorizo holds its shape and dices well. Sauté it to lend bold flavor to a bean and sausage stew such as Quick Chorizo and Morcilla Bean Stew (page 205).

BOTIFARRA

HOMEMADE SPICY LOOSE CATALAN SAUSAGE

MAKES THREE 1-POUND PORTIONS

2 tablespoons fennel seeds

2 tablespoons black peppercorns

½ teaspoon crushed red pepper

2 teaspoons kosher salt

3 pounds lean ground pork

1   Preheat the oven to 350°F.

2   Arrange the fennel seeds and peppercorns in a single layer on a sheet pan. Toast the spices until the fennel seeds are fragrant and golden brown all over, 8 to 10 minutes, shaking the pan once or twice. Let the spices cool completely, 5 to 7 minutes.

3   Transfer the toasted spices to a mortar or spice grinder and pound or pulse until just cracked. Transfer the cracked spices to a large bowl. Add the pepper flakes, salt, and the pork. Use your hands to mix thoroughly. Use the sausage immediately or divide it into 1-pound portions (or ½-pound portions if that is more convenient), wrap tightly in plastic, and refrigerate for up to 3 days or freeze for up to 3 months.

LA FAVADA RÀPIDA

QUICK CHORIZO AND
MORCILLA BEAN STEW

SERVES 4

This recipe turns *favada*, a traditionally slow-cooked dish, into a quick stew with pork sausage and white beans. This is the sort of stew that sticks to your bones and makes you feel cozy on a cold winter night. While fresh *morcilla* and Spanish chorizo are typically used, Homemade Spicy Loose Catalan Sausage (page 203) would also be delicious here. Look for morcilla at a Hispanic market or order it online.

1½ cups cooked or canned white beans, drained and rinsed

3 tablespoons vegetable oil

1 tablespoon extra-virgin olive oil

1 ounce cansalada or slab bacon, finely chopped

4 links (3 ounces each) fresh Spanish chorizo sausages,
cut into ¼-inch pieces

4 morcilla or botifarra negra sausages (2 ounces each),
cut into ¼-inch pieces

2 tablespoons chopped garlic

2 tablespoons Allioli (page 32) or store-bought aioli

2 cups Chicken, Beef, or Pork Stock (page 35) or store-bought stock

1 tablespoon chopped fresh curly parsley

2 teaspoons pimentón (smoked paprika)

Kosher salt

1   Add ¼ cup of the white beans to a mortar. Use a pestle to break and pound the beans to a thick paste. Set aside.

2   In a large Dutch oven, heat the oils over medium-high heat. When the oil is shimmering, add the *cansalada* and cook, stirring, until the fat is rendered, 1 to 2 minutes. Stir in the chorizo pieces and cook until warmed through, about 1 minute. Add the morcilla and garlic and cook until the garlic begins to turn golden brown, about 1 minute, stirring. Stir in the remaining cooked beans, and then the reserved mashed beans. Stir in the allioli and stock, mixing all the ingredients together. Simmer until the broth has thickened a bit, 3 to 4 minutes.

3   Remove the pot from the heat, and stir in the parsley and pimentón. Taste and season with salt, if needed.

MANDONGUILLES AMB SÍPIA
MEATBALLS WITH CUTTLEFISH

SERVES 4
AS A FIRST COURSE
OR TAPA

In Catalonia, we often eat this classic combination for lunch alongside some rice. It is usually served in its pan gravy with some fresh peas. This simplicity allows you to taste the Catalan countryside in the pork meatballs as well as the Mediterranean coast in the cuttlefish. It is such a familiar example of *mar i muntanya* (see page 172) that I sometimes call it by that name out of habit.

MANDONGUILLES (MEATBALLS)

1½ teaspoons fennel seeds

1 tablespoon pine nuts

12 ounces ground pork

2 tablespoons chopped fresh cilantro

2 tablespoons chopped fresh mint

1 small egg, beaten

2 tablespoons fine breadcrumbs

½ teaspoon kosher salt

PICADA

10 roasted almonds, roughly chopped

2 garlic cloves, roughly chopped

Kosher salt

1 tablespoon chopped fresh curly parsley

2 tablespoons fine breadcrumbs

TO FINISH

¼ cup extra-virgin olive oil

4 ounces cuttlefish, cut into 1-inch pieces (see note)

2 tablespoons Sofregit (page 34) or store-bought sofrito

1½ cups Vegetable Stock (page 35) or store-bought vegetable stock

¼ cup frozen peas, thawed

Kosher salt

EL CONSELL: Look for cuttlefish at an Asian market or specialty store. If you have trouble finding it, squid steaks make a great substitute.

1 Prepare the *mandonguilles*: Preheat the oven to 350°F.

2 Arrange the fennel seeds on one side of a sheet pan and the pine nuts on the other. Bake until they are golden and fragrant, 7 to 8 minutes, tossing each on its own side halfway through. Set the pan aside until both are cool. Transfer the toasted fennel seeds to a mortar or spice grinder and pound or pulse until just cracked.

3 In a large bowl, combine the cracked fennel seeds, pine nuts, pork, cilantro, mint, egg, breadcrumbs, and salt. Mix together using your hands until completely combined. Portion the meat into twelve 1-ounce pieces (about 1 heaping tablespoon) and gently roll into balls.

4 Make the *picada*: Mash together the almonds, garlic, and a generous pinch of salt to a fine paste in a mortar with a pestle. Gradually add the parsley, mashing to a fine paste. Stir in the breadcrumbs.

5 Finish the dish: In a large skillet, heat the oil over medium heat. When the oil is shimmering, add the meatballs and brown all over, about 10 minutes, turning occasionally. Add the cuttlefish and cook until it shrinks and turns opaque, 1 to 2 minutes, tossing frequently.

6 Stir in the picada, sofregit, and stock, breaking up the picada with a spoon as it comes to a simmer. Cook until the sauce thickens to the consistency of heavy cream, about 10 minutes, rolling the meatballs through the sauce occasionally. Stir in the peas and cook until heated through, 2 to 3 minutes. Season with salt to taste.

7 Serve the meatballs and cuttlefish in shallow bowls with the pan sauce spooned over the top.

PEUS DE PORC

PIGS' FEET TERRINE IN MUSTARD SAUCE

Pigs' feet are a natural go-to meat in the humble culinary traditions of Catalans. We appreciate the entire animal, and stewing the tough cuts renders them perfectly soft and succulent. This preparation is one I adapted and refined for people living outside of Catalonia who may not be familiar with this cut of pork. For you who have never tried pigs' feet, here is your dish. The gristle and bones have been removed, leaving the luscious meat a pure pleasure to eat. The pigs' feet cook slowly for several hours, so get the dish going in the afternoon before your evening meal. I like to serve this terrine with steamed haricot verts (thin green beans).

¼ cup extra-virgin olive oil

1 medium yellow onion, chopped

1 small leek, halved lengthwise and sliced

Kosher salt

½ large apple, chopped

¼ small bulb fennel, cored and sliced

1 cup dry white wine

3 bay leaves

12 black peppercorns

1 star anise

3 sprigs fresh thyme

¼ bunch fresh curly parsley sprigs

2 whole front legs of pork (about 3 pounds total), halved (see note) and rinsed

About 6 cups Chicken or Pork Stock (page 35) or store-bought stock

2 tablespoons salted butter, cut into pieces

3 tablespoons finely chopped shallots

1 tablespoon chopped fresh tarragon

1 cup Mustard Sauce (page 132)

1 Preheat the oven to 300°F.

2 In a large roasting pan, heat the oil over medium heat. When the oil is shimmering, add the onion and leek, season with salt, and reduce the heat to medium-low. Cook until the vegetables soften and begin to release their liquid, about 10 minutes, stirring occasionally. Add the apple, fennel, and wine and cook until the apple and fennel soften and the wine reduces in volume by about half, about 10 minutes, stirring once or twice. Add the bay leaves, peppercorns, star anise, thyme, and parsley. Add the pork legs to the pan, spooning some vegetables onto the meat. Pour in enough stock to cover and submerge the meat. Increase the heat to high and bring to a boil.

3 Cover the roasting pan with foil and transfer to the oven. Bake until the meat begins falling from the bone, about 4 hours. Remove the pan from the oven.

4   Lift the pork legs from the liquid and transfer to a sheet pan to cool until just
    warm, about 30 minutes. When the pork is warm to the touch, carefully pull
    the skin away from legs and set it aside on a cutting board—try not to rip the
    skin when pulling it from the meat. Use the flat side of a knife to scrape the
    underside of the pork skin of excess fat, discarding the fat. Chop the skin very
    finely. Pull the meat from the bone, then roughly chop the meat.

5   Set a medium bowl into a larger bowl filled with ice. Strain the roasting pan
    contents through a fine-mesh strainer into the medium bowl, discarding the
    solids. As the broth cools in the bowl, a layer of fat will rise to the top; skim it
    off and discard it. Measure out 3 cups of the skimmed broth and transfer to a
    large saucepan (reserving the remaining broth). Bring to a boil over high heat
    and cook until the broth reduces in volume by one-third, 10 to 12 minutes.

6   Preheat the oven to 400°F.

7   In a medium saucepan, melt the butter over medium heat. When the butter
    is foamy, add the shallot, season with salt, and reduce the heat to medium-
    low. Cook until translucent, 2 to 3 minutes. Stir in the tarragon and chopped
    pork skin and cook until the fat is rendered and the shallots become glossy,
    about 5 minutes, stirring often. Stir in the reserved meat and about 1 cup of
    the remaining broth. Cook until the mixture becomes very dense, sticky to the
    touch, and glued together, about 10 minutes.

8   Place eight 4- to 5-ounce ramekins on a sheet pan. Fill the ramekins with the
    meat mixture, transfer to the oven, and roast until they are heated through,
    10 to 12 minutes. Drizzle each ramekin with mustard sauce and serve warm.

EL CONSELL: Look for the pork legs at a farmer's market. Ask the butcher to cut
and clean the pork for you. Or, if you have a heavy cleaver, you can do it yourself.

LLOM DE PORC CANARI
SLOW-ROASTED PORK LOIN

Pork loins are often sautéed or grilled over high heat, which cooks the lean meat a bit too aggressively for my taste. Here's a different way to cook a pork loin—brined, rubbed with a spice blend typical of the Canary Islands, then gently roasted. The roasted loin is chilled, thinly sliced, and served like carpaccio with some bracing pickled onions and rich, fruity olive oil. Sometimes I add watercress or other greens to the plate, simply dressed with cava vinegar, olive oil, salt, and pepper. Brining the pork and chilling it after it's cooked takes several hours, so start the dish the morning before you serve it, or even a couple days before.

6 tablespoons kosher salt

1 tablespoon sugar

⅓ cup honey

2 ancho chiles

3 garlic cloves, smashed, plus 6 cloves, chopped

2 bay leaves

¾ teaspoon black peppercorns

¾ teaspoon coriander seeds

¾ teaspoon crushed red pepper

¼ teaspoon plus 2 tablespoons pimentón (smoked paprika)

¼ cup packed fresh curly parsley leaves and stems

6 cups ice cubes

1 center-cut pork loin roast (3 to 4 pounds), trimmed

2 tablespoons fresh rosemary leaves

1 teaspoon fresh thyme leaves

⅓ cup extra-virgin olive oil, plus more for serving

½ cup Pickled Red Onions (recipe follows), for serving

Flaky sea salt, for serving

1 In a large stockpot, combine 3 cups water, the salt, and sugar. Bring to a simmer over high heat, stirring until the salt and sugar dissolve. Reduce the heat to medium-low and stir in the honey, chiles, 3 smashed garlic cloves, 1 bay leaf, peppercorns, coriander, red pepper flakes, ¼ teaspoon pimentón, and the parsley. Remove the pot from the heat and add the ice, stirring until it melts and the brine is cool to the touch, 1 to 2 minutes. Add the pork loin to the brine and submerge it. Cover, transfer the pot to the refrigerator, and brine the pork for at least 6 hours or overnight.

2 Preheat the oven to 350°F.

3 Remove the pork from the brine and pat dry (discard the brine). Use kitchen twine to tie the pork in 6 to 8 places, making the roast into a compact cylinder. Place the remaining bay leaf in a mortar or spice grinder and pound or pulse until finely ground. Transfer it to a small bowl and add the rosemary, thyme, 6 cloves chopped garlic, and remaining 2 tablespoons pimentón. Stir in the oil to create a thick paste. Rub the paste all over the pork.

(recipe continues)

4   Transfer the pork to a rack set in a roasting pan. Roast until a thermometer inserted into the thickest part of the pork reads 125°F, 30 to 40 minutes. Set the pork aside on a rack to cool to room temperature, about 1 hour. When the pork is cool, wrap it in plastic and refrigerate until chilled through, at least 1 hour or up to 2 days.

5   To serve, use a sharp, thin knife to slice the pork as thinly as possible, removing the twine as you slice. Overlap the pork slices to cover the bottoms of four plates. Scatter on the pickled onions, drizzle with olive oil, and sprinkle with flaky salt. Serve chilled.

EL CONSELL: I like to sandwich a few slices of this pork on some bread with the pickled onions. You can also make a *pinxto*: Place a slice of pork on a work surface, scatter some pickled onions over it, roll it tightly, and skewer it with a toothpick. Drizzle with oil and sprinkle with flaky sea salt before serving.

CEBES VERMELLES ESCABETXADES
PICKLED RED ONIONS

MAKES 3 CUPS

1 cup red wine vinegar

1 cup cava vinegar or champagne vinegar

1 cup sugar

4 dried cayenne-type chiles

6 star anise

2 teaspoons coriander seeds

6 bay leaves

Kosher salt

2 medium red onions, halved and very thinly sliced

1   In a medium saucepan, combine both vinegars, 2 cups water, the sugar, chiles, star anise, coriander seeds, bay leaves, and a few generous pinches of salt. Bring to a boil over high heat, reduce the heat to low, and simmer, stirring occasionally, until the sugar is dissolved, 3 to 4 minutes.

2   Place the onions in a large heatproof bowl and pour the hot brine over them. Set aside to cool and pickle for at least 1 hour. Store the onions in their brine in an airtight container in the refrigerator for up to 1 week. The flavor will improve the longer the onions are left to pickle.

MACARRONS COM A CASA

PENNE PASTA WITH HOMEMADE BACON AND TOMATO SAUCE

SERVES 8
AS A MAIN DISH

Having evolved over hundreds of years, pasta dishes are traditional in Spain, and especially in Catalonia in the form of *fideuà* (Fideo Noodle Paella, page 133) and *canelons* (Brisket Canelones, page 192). The sauce on this baked pasta is almost gravy—it tastes distinctly Spanish from the sofregit and bacon. Adding a dash of hot sauce gives it extra bite (my favorite is El Yucateco "Salsa Picante de Chile Habanero"). Make this dish in advance, store it in the refrigerator or freezer, and reheat it for a hungry crowd.

4 tablespoons (½ stick) salted butter, plus more for greasing

1 pound dried penne pasta

1 small yellow onion, finely chopped

¼ cup all-purpose flour

2 cups whole milk

Kosher salt

1 teaspoon freshly grated nutmeg

2 ounces dried porcini or shiitake mushrooms, broken into small pieces

1 cup boiling water

1 tablespoon vegetable oil

4 ounces Homemade Bacon (recipe follows), or pancetta, cut into ¼-inch pieces

6 ounces sliced mixed fresh mushrooms, such as oyster, portobello, and shiitake

4 garlic cloves, finely chopped

1½ cups Sofregit (page 34) or store-bought sofrito

Dash of hot sauce (optional)

4 ounces Manchego cheese, coarsely grated

1 Preheat the oven to 400°F. Grease a 13 × 9-inch baking dish.

2 Bring a large pot of salted water to a boil over high heat. Add the penne and cook to al dente, 8 to 10 minutes. Drain and set aside.

3 While the pasta is cooking, in a medium saucepan, melt the butter over medium heat. When the butter is foamy, add the onion and reduce the heat to medium-low. Cook slowly until the onion is translucent, about 15 minutes, stirring. Whisk in the flour and cook until it bubbles and sizzles in the pan, about 5 minutes, stirring once or twice. Add the milk and bring the sauce to a simmer, whisking almost constantly until it thickens into béchamel, 2 to 3 minutes. Stir in 1 teaspoon salt and the nutmeg. Remove the béchamel from the heat.

4 Meanwhile, place the dried mushrooms in a small bowl and add the boiling water to cover. Let stand until the mushrooms swell significantly and the water is dark and fragrant, about 15 minutes. Pluck out the mushrooms, squeezing to fully extract the liquid. Set aside the mushrooms and soaking liquid separately. Rinse the mushrooms to be sure they are free of grit.

5 In a large skillet, heat the oil over medium-high heat. When the oil is shimmering, add the bacon and cook, stirring, until it begins to crisp, about 5 minutes. Add the fresh mushrooms, soaked mushrooms, and garlic. Cook, tossing, until all the mushrooms shrink and the garlic begins to brown, about 5 minutes. Pour the reserved mushroom soaking liquid through a small strainer to catch any grit, straining the liquid directly into the pan. Stir in the sofregit and hot sauce (if using), and simmer until thickened slightly, about 5 minutes. Add the cooked pasta and toss to combine.

6 Transfer the mixture to the baking dish. Spoon the béchamel over the pasta, then scatter the Manchego on top. Bake until browned and bubbling, 30 to 40 minutes. Let stand for 10 minutes before serving.

CANSALADA
HOMEMADE BACON

MAKES 1 POUND

10 dried bay leaves
2 star anise
2 tablespoons black peppercorns
2 cups kosher salt
1 cup granulated sugar
¼ cup finely chopped fresh rosemary leaves
4 large garlic cloves, finely chopped
2 tablespoons pink curing salt (optional)
1 large (3-pound) piece pork belly

1 In a mortar or spice grinder, combine the bay leaves, star anise, and peppercorns and pound or pulse until ground. Transfer to a large, shallow dish and add the salt, sugar, rosemary, garlic, and curing salt (if using).

2 Bury the pork belly in the seasoning mixture, caking the meat with it on all sides. Press plastic wrap onto the surface of the meat and place a heavy pan on top to weight it down. Refrigerate for at least 12 days or up to 3 weeks. The fat of the bacon should go from translucent to cloudy white, resembling stone.

3 Rinse and dry the meat well. Once cured, the slab of bacon can be used immediately or wrapped tightly in plastic and stored in a resealable bag in the refrigerator for up to 1 week or in the freezer for up to 3 months.

COSTELLES DE PORC AGREDOLCES

SWEET AND SOUR PORK RIBS

SERVES 4
AS A MAIN DISH
OR 8 TO 10 AS A TAPA

These pork ribs are similar to what Texans would identify as barbecue, although they are baked in the oven instead of smoked in a smoker. In Catalonia, a small plate of ribs is often served after a soup such as Gazpacho (page 86), especially in the summer, and they typically accompany a big salad in the middle of the table. You could also serve them as a main dish with a side of Wrinkly Potatoes (page 95).

About 4 pounds lard

2 racks (3 pounds each) St. Louis-style pork spareribs, trimmed (see note)

Kosher salt

2 tablespoons black peppercorns

4 bay leaves

1 cup extra-virgin olive oil

8 garlic cloves, very thinly sliced

1½ cups Barbecue Sauce (recipe follows)

1   Preheat the oven to 250°F.

2   In a roasting pan large enough to hold the spareribs, melt the lard over medium heat. Generously season both sides of the ribs with salt. Add them to the pan, submerging them completely in the lard. Add the peppercorns and bay leaves, and cover the pan tightly with foil. Transfer it to the oven and bake until the meat is very tender and pulls away easily from the bone, 2½ to 3 hours.

3   Meanwhile, in a small saucepan, heat the olive oil over medium heat. When the oil is shimmering, add the garlic, stirring constantly to be sure the garlic swims freely in the oil. Reduce the heat to low and cook until the garlic chips are evenly golden brown and they sizzle less aggressively, 6 to 8 minutes. Drain the chips in a small colander set over a bowl, reserving the garlic-flavored oil in a glass mason jar (it will keep for several weeks in the refrigerator). Turn the garlic chips out onto paper towels to drain and season with salt.

4   When the ribs are done, transfer them to a cutting board to cool slightly.

5   Heat the broiler with a rack in the highest position in the oven. Line a sheet pan with foil.

(recipe continues)

6   When the pork is cool enough to handle, slice between the bones to cut the racks into individual ribs. Brush both sides of the ribs with barbecue sauce to coat completely. Arrange on the lined sheet pan and broil until the sauce is thick and sticky to the touch, about 2 minutes. Flip the ribs with tongs, brush with more sauce, and continue broiling until the sauce begins to char in spots, about 2 minutes more. Sprinkle the ribs with the garlic chips and serve immediately.

EL CONSELL: The sheer white membrane from the underside (bone-side) of each rack of ribs should be removed because it can toughen during cooking. To remove it, use a paper towel to grab the membrane from one corner. It should peel off like a like a tough sticker.

SALSA BARBACOA
BARBECUE SAUCE

MAKES ABOUT 1½ CUPS

3 tablespoons extra-virgin olive oil

1 medium yellow onion, chopped

4 garlic cloves, chopped

2 tablespoons whiskey

1 cup ketchup

3 tablespoons light brown sugar

3 tablespoons apple cider vinegar

3 tablespoons Worcestershire sauce

1 tablespoon Dijon mustard

1   In a medium saucepan, heat the oil over medium-high heat. When the oil is shimmering, add the onion, reduce the heat to medium, and cook until the onion is almost translucent, about 10 minutes, stirring occasionally. Stir in the garlic and cook until fragrant and softened, about 3 minutes, stirring often. Increase the heat to high, stir in the whiskey, and cook until the whiskey almost completely evaporates, about 5 minutes. Add the ketchup, brown sugar, vinegar, Worcestershire sauce, and mustard and stir as the sauce comes to a boil. Reduce the heat to low and simmer until the sauce thickens to the consistency of ketchup, 5 to 10 minutes more.

2   Transfer to a food processor or blender (pulling out the center cap from the lid to allow steam to escape if using a blender), and carefully puree until smooth. (Alternatively, use an immersion blender to blend in the pan until smooth.) Store the sauce in glass jars or containers in the refrigerator for up to 3 weeks.

LLOM DE PORC IBÈRIC A LA PLANXA

SEARED IBÉRICO TENDERLOIN WITH CHORIZO MIGAS

SERVES 6

AS A MAIN DISH

The Ibérico tenderloin, like the *secreto* Ibérico (see page 226), is one of those cuts that the families who raised Ibérico pigs would keep for themselves. I didn't even taste it until I befriended a US purveyor. After tasting it, I got inspired to cook with it. My San Francisco chef-friend, Ritsu Tsuchida, makes amazing Japanese ramen, and he inspired me to combine this Spanish cut of meat with Castilian *migas* (breadcrumbs and chorizo), as well as Japanese miso, mirin, and sake. The rich, nutty-tasting meat pairs perfectly with bracing and savory Japanese flavors.

½ cup panko breadcrumbs

2 tablespoons plus 2 teaspoons olive oil, plus more to finish

Kosher salt

2 cups mirin

2 cups sake

½ cup red miso paste

2 Ibérico pork tenderloins (12 ounces each), each trimmed and cut into 3 medallions (see note)

½ cup finely chopped red bell pepper

½ cup finely chopped green bell pepper

1 link (4 ounces) Spanish chorizo, such as Riojano, casing removed and finely chopped

Flaky sea salt, for serving

1 Preheat the oven to 350°F.

2 On a large sheet pan, toss the panko with 2 teaspoons of the olive oil and a pinch of salt. Toast until golden brown, 8 to 10 minutes, shaking the pan occasionally. Set aside.

3 Meanwhile, in a medium saucepan, bring the mirin and sake to a simmer over medium-high heat. Cook until the liquid reduces by about half, about 15 minutes. Set aside to cool completely, about 30 minutes. Whisk in the miso.

4 Pour the marinade into a resealable plastic bag and add the pork. Turn to coat, press out the air, seal, and marinate in the refrigerator for 1½ hours.

(recipe continues)

5   Heat a large nonstick skillet over medium-high heat. Coat the pork with 1 tablespoon of the olive oil and sprinkle all over with salt. When the skillet is just smoking, working with one piece at a time, add the pork and quickly sear until the surface is opaque and lightly browned, about 2 minutes per side. Set aside on plates.

6   Add the remaining 1 tablespoon olive oil to the pan. When the oil is shimmering, add the bell peppers and chorizo and cook until the peppers are tender and the chorizo begins to brown, 3 to 5 minutes, stirring now and then.

7   Scatter the toasted panko onto six dinner plates. Arrange the pork over the panko and spoon on the chorizo mixture. Drizzle everything with olive oil and sprinkle with flaky salt.

EL CONSELL: Look for Ibérico pork tenderloins online or at specialty Spanish grocers (see Resources on page 266). Though their flavor and marbling cannot be compared, this recipe will work with standard pork tenderloin.

CANSALADA A LA PLANXA

BEER-BRAISED CRISPY PORK BELLY

SERVES 8 TO 10
AS A FIRST COURSE

A typical Catalan breakfast consists of a thick slice of *cansalada*, or pork belly, cooked on a *planxa* or cast-iron plank and served alongside grilled sardines and Catalan Tomato Bread (page 38). This dish uses a seared slab of cansalada but brings it to the dinner table with a bit more elegance. To serve it as part of a family-style Catalan feast, match it with Penne Pasta with Homemade Bacon and Tomato Sauce (page 214) and Octopus with Caramelized Onion Tomato Sauce (page 145), as well as Catalan Tomato Bread. Make it the day before so it has time to chill. You could even refrigerate it for up to 1 week or freeze it for up to 3 months. Then you can simply sear off the cubes of pork belly and reheat the braising liquid for serving.

1 slab (3 pounds) pork belly, preferably skin-on

Kosher salt and freshly ground black pepper

2 tablespoons vegetable oil

2 medium carrots, peeled and sliced on the diagonal

1 medium yellow onion, halved and thinly sliced

1 medium apple, peeled and chopped

1 medium shallot, chopped

1 star anise

2 whole cloves

1 tablespoon coriander seeds

2 bottles (12 ounces each) porter or stout (see note)

About 8 cups Pork or Chicken Stock (page 35) or store-bought stock

2 green onions (green and white parts), thinly sliced on the diagonal

Finely grated fresh horseradish, for serving

1   Preheat the oven to 250°F.

2   Season both sides of the pork belly generously with salt and pepper.

3   In a large Dutch oven, heat the oil over medium heat. When the oil is shimmering, add the carrots, onion, apple, and shallot and season with salt. Reduce the heat to medium-low and cook until the vegetables begin to release liquid, about 10 minutes, stirring often. Stir in the star anise, cloves, and coriander seeds, and cook until fragrant, about 1 minute.

EL NOSTRE AMIC, EL PORC

224

4 Pour in the beer, then nestle the pork belly in among the vegetables. Pour enough stock over the meat to cover and submerge it. Increase the heat to high and bring to a boil. Cover and transfer to the oven. Braise until the pork is very tender, 3 to 4 hours. Remove the pork from the oven and leave the oven on but increase the oven temperature to 475°F.

5 Lift the pork from the braising liquid and transfer the pork to a sheet pan. Pour the braising liquid through a fine-mesh strainer into a medium saucepan. Discard the solids.

6 Return the pork on the sheet pan to the oven and roast until the surface is evenly golden brown, sizzling, and crisp, 5 to 8 minutes. Set aside to cool to room temperature. When cooled, refrigerate the pork until thoroughly chilled, about 1 hour.

7 When ready to serve, cut the cold pork into 1- to 1½-inch cubes. You will have about 30 pieces. Heat a large cast-iron skillet over medium heat. Add the pork cubes and brown them all over, about 2 minutes per side. Reheat the braising liquid.

8 Serve the pork in shallow bowls with the warm braising liquid. Top with the green onions and scatter the fresh horseradish over the top.

EL CONSELL: Choose a beer for braising the pork that isn't too bitter, such as a vanilla porter.

SECRET IBÈRIC A LA PLANXA
GRIDDLED SECRETO IBÉRICO

The *secreto* is like the skirt steak of an Ibérico pig, cut from the diaphragm muscles. I discovered it after I moved to the United States because back in Spain, you generally don't eat odd cuts of Ibérico unless you've raised the pigs yourself. It is so rich and tender after cooking that it melts in your mouth like a prized piece of toro at the best sushi restaurant. I like to serve it over a warm bed of cauliflower puree topped with a salad of sliced celery, toasted hazelnuts, and chopped parsley dressed with olive oil and cava vinegar.

PORK

1 pound secreto Ibérico, cut into four 4-ounce pieces, trimmed

4 garlic cloves, finely chopped

1 tablespoon finely chopped fresh rosemary

1 tablespoon extra-virgin olive oil

1 tablespoon soy sauce

1 teaspoon crushed red pepper

Kosher salt and freshly ground black pepper

CAULIFLOWER PUREE

1 medium head cauliflower (about 2 pounds), leaves trimmed

2 tablespoons extra-virgin olive oil

Kosher salt and freshly ground black pepper

3 garlic cloves, peeled

About ½ cup heavy cream

Celery Salad (recipe follows)

Extra-virgin olive oil, for drizzling

Flaky sea salt, for serving

1 Marinate the pork: Combine the pork, garlic, rosemary, oil, soy sauce, and pepper flakes in a resealable plastic bag. Season with salt and black pepper and shake to combine, then seal and marinate overnight in the refrigerator.

2 Prepare the cauliflower puree: Preheat the oven to 400°F.

3 Place the cauliflower on a large piece of foil and rub the oil all over it. Season all over with salt and pepper and add the garlic to the foil. Wrap the cauliflower and garlic in the foil. Bake until the cauliflower is fork-tender and the garlic is golden brown, 40 to 45 minutes. Remove and let cool in the foil until cool enough to handle, 10 to 15 minutes. Unwrap the cauliflower, then cut out and discard the core. Coarsely chop the cauliflower and transfer it to a food processor along with the roasted garlic and any liquid left in the foil. Puree until smooth, adding enough cream to create a puree with the consistency of loose mashed potatoes, about 1 minute. Taste and season with salt and pepper if needed. Transfer to a small saucepan and keep warm over low heat, stirring occasionally to prevent sticking.

4 Remove the meat from the marinade and pat dry. Heat a large cast-iron skillet over medium-high heat. When the skillet is just smoking, add the meat, working in batches if necessary, and sear until deep golden brown on both sides, about 10 minutes total. Remove to a cutting board and let rest for a minute or so.

5 Thinly slice the pieces crosswise at a slight angle against the grain of the meat to create wide slices.

6 Spoon the warm cauliflower puree onto four plates. Top with the pork slices and the celery salad. Drizzle with olive oil, and sprinkle with flaky sea salt.

AMANIDA D'API
CELERY SALAD

SERVES 4

2 teaspoons cava vinegar or champagne vinegar
2 tablespoons extra-virgin olive oil
Kosher salt and freshly ground black pepper
1 celery rib, thinly sliced crosswise on the diagonal
½ cup loosely packed small fresh curly parsley leaves
¼ cup skinless hazelnuts, toasted and coarsely chopped

Pour the vinegar into a medium bowl. Whisk in the oil drop by drop at first, then in a slow, steady stream until the oil is incorporated into the vinegar and the mixture thickens, about 1 minute. Season with salt and pepper. Add the celery, parsley, and hazelnuts and toss to coat. Serve immediately.

PERMIL IBÈRIC

IBÉRICO HAM

Cured hams hang in almost every market shop window in Catalonia. In fact, ham is a specialty of the entire Iberian Peninsula, including Spain and Portugal. What is known as Serrano ham can be produced in every Spanish province from a variety of pork breeds. The most prized legs of *permil Ibèric*, however, are strictly regulated by the Spanish government to ensure authenticity.

Cerdo Ibérico is the breed of pig that produces Ibérico hams, and it originates in the mountainous region of southern Spain. Ibérico pigs date back to when Romans ruled the Iberian Peninsula, and this breed is highly prized for the fat-to-lean ratio of its meat. Though there are some breed variations (such as red and spotted), Ibérico pigs are most commonly recognized by their thin, dark coats; long, slender faces; pointed snouts; and black hooves, or *pata negra*. To be considered authentic, Ibérico ham must come from pigs with at least 75 percent pure Ibérico heritage.

The finest Ibérico pigs, classified as *bellota* (meaning "acorn"), are raised in regions of multipurpose agricultural pasture called *dehesa*, which are forested mainly with oak trees. During the autumn months, these pigs are released into the pasture to fatten on acorns; each pig eats about twenty-two pounds of acorns, gaining up to two pounds of fat per day for six months. To achieve bellota classification, Ibérico pigs must replace at least 60 percent of their body weight during this grazing period.

Just below the bellota classification of Ibérico pigs are the *recebo*, which means "gravel," an indication that the pigs were raised partially in the barnyard rather than in the forest. Recebo pigs are required to gain only 50 percent of their weight from acorns. The lowest classification is simply the Ibérico pig, which lacks a regulated grazing period and is permitted to crossbreed. It has only been possible to trace the classification of imported Ibérico ham in the US since 2007, which makes it difficult to authenticate the labels you see in markets. A conversation with a reputable importer will help.

On a microscopic level, the diet of Ibérico pigs (particularly the bellota classification) affects the curing process and the taste of the meat itself. Antioxidants in acorns act as natural preservatives that aid the salt-curing process. The animal's diet actually helps prevent the meat from going rancid as it hangs and dries in the autumn and winter. In the warmer months, fat gradually melts from the ham, resulting in drier cured meat with a more concentrated nutty flavor. This later stage of the curing process—sometimes referred to as "sweating"—causes the leg's fat to remain softer at room temperature. That's why the good stuff glistens on the plate and melts in your mouth.

The complete curing process takes place over several seasons and varies according to the weight of the leg being cured and the mastery of the person curing it. Traditionally, a *bodega* (finishing cellar) as well as its *cansalader* (master meat curer) determines the final flavor of the ham sold. The craftsmanship and artistry of the process help to explain why prices of Ibérico ham vary so widely.

To showcase the refined qualities of the finest Ibérico hams, the legs are always stored at room temperature in a sturdy ham holder and thinly sliced by hand using a long, slim blade. Paper-thin, bite-size slices are best served in a single layer, traditionally on barely warmed plates to soften the flavorful fat and open up the meat's complex aromas.

PA I POSTRES
BREAD AND DESSERTS

To cap off weekday meals in Catalonia, it is very typical to enjoy a simple dessert of ripe fruit or another *sobretaula* ("on top of the table") to nibble on as the table conversation continues. On Sundays, however, ladies will get dressed up to shop at the local bakery for a nice cake. We have such fantastic *pastisseries* and *fleques* (pastry shops and bakeries) in Catalonia that most home cooks leave the fancy desserts to the professionals. However, some of these sweets are easily made at home. I also like to make fresh bread and have included a simple, country-style loaf made in a cast-iron Dutch oven.

COCA DOLÇA
SWEET CATALAN FLATBREAD

MAKES **6**
FLATBREADS

These flatbreads are sold by weight at every corner bakery in Catalonia. At room temperature, they pair perfectly with afternoon coffee. For proper *coca*, stretch the dough very thin and add the toppings with a generous hand. Pine nuts and sugar are customary, but feel free to experiment with your favorite additions.

¾ cup warm whole milk

¾ cup warm water

¾ cup cup sugar

¾ teaspoon active dry yeast

¼ cup extra-virgin olive oil, plus more for drizzling

1 cup semolina flour

3 cups all-purpose flour

1 teaspoon ground cinnamon

¾ teaspoon kosher salt

½ cup pine nuts, toasted

Lemon zest, for serving

1 In a stand mixer fitted with the dough hook, combine the milk, water, ¼ cup of the sugar, the yeast, and olive oil. Let stand until frothy, about 10 minutes.

2 In a medium bowl, combine the semolina flour, all-purpose flour, cinnamon, and salt. Add the flour mixture to the yeast mixture, and mix on medium speed until the dough forms a tight ball around the dough hook, about 7 minutes. Use a bench scraper or silicone spatula to gather it into a compact ball.

3 Drizzle a large bowl with a bit of olive oil and add the dough. Drizzle some additional oil over the dough, spreading a thin coating over its surface with your hand. Cover the bowl with a damp towel and set it aside in a warm spot to rise to roughly double its size, about 2 hours. If you have time, let the dough rest overnight in the refrigerator for even more flavor. It will also be easier to roll out the next day.

4 Divide the dough into 6 equal pieces and transfer to a parchment-lined sheet pan. Let the dough stand for 10 minutes in a warm place before rolling it out.

5 Preheat the oven to 425°F. Position racks in the upper and lower thirds of the oven. Line two sheet pans with parchment paper.

6 On a floured work surface, roll out each piece of dough into an oval about 8 inches long. Transfer the ovals to the prepared sheet pans as they are shaped. Sprinkle the dough with the pine nuts and the remaining ½ cup sugar.

7 Bake until puffed and browned around the edges, about 12 minutes total. Halfway through the baking, switch the pans between the racks and rotate the pans from front to back for even browning. While the flatbreads are still warm, grate the lemon zest on top. Slice each in half and pile on a plate.

BREAD AND DESSERTS

233

EL PA DE CADA DIA

OUR DAILY BREAD

A staple of Catalan cuisine, bread is rooted in peasant culture, as it fills the gaps left by meager portions of meat, fish, and other more expensive foods.

Bread is such a vital part of the Catalan diet that each household usually has a consistent bread order that does not change from day to day. In fact, the bakery is the only shop Catalans visit every day. Traditionally, each household has its own *coixinera* (bread bag) left in care of the bakery cashier to fill with the standard house order of bread. *Coixinera* translates to "pillowcase," so called because of its resemblance to bed linens. However, these bags are made of special fabric that maintains the optimal humidity to slow the staling process and help preserve the bread. In most home kitchens, you will see hooks expressly for hanging filled coixinera right alongside the empty ones destined for a return trip to the bakery. As part of the local honor system, you pay for your bread at the end of the week according to your total number of coixinera refills.

Bread is so revered in Catalonia that you never waste even a single slice. It is served with several dishes, such as paella, and it is snuck into others, as in the breadcrumbs used to bind meatballs (Meatballs with Cuttlefish, page 206) and the breadcrumbs bulking up *picadas* in dishes like Stewed Chickpeas with Spinach (page 101). To dress up the odd slice of bread, a variety of snacks have evolved, including bread with olive oil and sea salt, *pa amb tomaquet* (Catalan Tomato Bread, page 38), bread with chocolate, and *pa amb vi i sucre* (Bread with Wine and Sugar, page 239). If the bread does go stale, most home cooks will make bread soup, which starts with garlic fried in olive oil to which pieces of stale bread are added along with a scrambled egg, sometimes a little fresh thyme, and then enough stock poured into the pot to make a soft and spoonable soup served in bowls with a heavy drizzle of olive oil and a pinch of pimentón.

For many restaurants and households, the quantity of bread in a meal tends to be a bigger concern than the quality. Bread from the corner *fleca* (bakery) typically has a fluffy, refined texture and lacks the signature chew considered standard for artisanal loaves elsewhere. Bread is simply considered a necessity in Catalonia. In fact, if the fleca sells you a small loaf of bread that is underweight, it is customary for the bakery cashier to weigh your loaf and give you a chunk from another loaf, called *la torna* (the "return") to make up the full kilo.

PA DE PAGÈS

FARMER'S BREAD

For most Catalans, good bread is only as far away as the corner store. However, it's not as convenient for farmers, who often make a large loaf like this to last the week. This recipe was inspired by a Vilafranca baker and friend of mine, Marc Parés, who runs the excellent Fleca Parés with his brother, Gaby. They use a sourdough starter, but I simply capture the flavor with a long fermentation time. I also use Jim Lahey's well-known cast-iron baking method for good results in a home oven. The dough ferments for 12 hours, so start this recipe a day ahead.

360 grams (2⅔ cups) bread flour

3 grams (1 teaspoon) active dry yeast

360 grams (1½ cups) water at 55°F

6 grams (2 teaspoons) kosher salt

50 grams (½ cup) rye flour, plus more for shaping

1 In the bowl of a stand mixer, combine the bread flour, yeast, water, and salt. Cover the bowl and set aside until the mixture doubles in bulk, looks bubbly, and smells pleasantly sour, 12 to 15 hours.

2 Attach the dough hook to the stand mixer. Scatter the 50 grams (½ cup) rye flour over the dough and knead with the dough hook on medium speed until it develops thick, sturdy strands that envelop the hook and adhere to the sides of the bowl, about 10 minutes, stopping once to scrape down the sides.

3 Place a small pile of rye flour (about ⅓ cup) on a piece of parchment. Turn the dough out onto the floured parchment, then fold and shape the dough with damp hands into a compact ball. Cover with a damp kitchen towel and let the dough rise on the parchment in a warm spot until doubled in bulk, about 1 hour. It will splay out in an odd mass as it grows.

4 While the dough rises again, set a medium cast-iron Dutch oven (with its lid in place) on the center rack of the oven and preheat the oven to 500°F.

5 Score the surface of the dough with a thin, sharp knife. Carefully and quickly remove the lid from the preheated pan and use the parchment to lift and lower the dough into the hot pan, still on the parchment. Cover the pot, return it to the oven, and reduce the temperature to 450°F. Bake until the loaf is risen but only lightly browned, about 30 minutes. Uncover and bake until the loaf develops a deep brown crust, 20 to 35 minutes more. Use the parchment to transfer the loaf to a cooling rack, remove the parchment, and let the bread cool completely, at least 30 minutes, before slicing.

PA AMB VI I SUCRE
BREAD WITH WINE AND SUGAR

This dish is something my grandmother used to make for me as a *berenar*, an evening snack, when I was a kid. It's a thrifty way to enjoy stale bread: Drown a slice in red wine and sprinkle it handsomely with sugar. While I still love to eat the rustic version, this recipe from my friend, the baker Marc Parés, translates those flavors into a slightly more dressed-up dessert in the form of individual spice cakes dipped in wine syrup and rolled in sugar.

½ cup red wine

¾ cup granulated sugar

1 cup honey

¼ cup packed light brown sugar

1 cup all-purpose flour

1 cup rye flour

2½ teaspoons baking powder

2½ teaspoons ground cinnamon

2½ teaspoons freshly grated nutmeg

¼ teaspoon ground aniseed

¼ teaspoon ground cloves

½ cup whole milk

2 large eggs

Gently whipped crème fraîche, for serving

1 Position a rack in the center of the oven and preheat to 350°F. Place twelve 2¾-inch paper baking molds on a sheet pan or line a 12-cup muffin tin with paper liners.

2 In a small saucepan, combine the wine and ½ cup of the granulated sugar. Bring to a boil over medium-high heat, stirring to dissolve the sugar. Remove the pan from the heat and let the syrup cool completely, at least 20 minutes.

3 In a small bowl, whisk together the honey and brown sugar.

4 Sift together the flours, baking powder, and spices into a large bowl. Make a well in the center of the sifted mixture and add the milk and eggs. Whisk the milk and eggs together, incorporating the dry ingredients as they are pulled into the well. Whisk in the honey mixture until a batter forms.

5 Divide the batter among the paper molds or muffin cups, filling each two-thirds of the way. Bake until the cakes have domed, slightly cracked, and turned golden brown on top, 20 to 25 minutes. Transfer to a wire rack to cool completely.

6 Place the remaining ¼ cup granulated sugar in a medium shallow bowl.

7 Just before serving, dunk the top of each cake into the wine syrup so it soaks in a little. Roll the sides of the soaked cakes through the sugar. Serve with a dollop of crème fraîche and an extra drizzle of wine syrup.

XURROS AMB XOCOLATA

CHURROS WITH HOT CHOCOLATE

These *xurros* are similar to the Mexican version you may know already from street fairs, but extra decadent since the dough includes butter and eggs. And they are made in no time on the stovetop. To get your xurros nice and crisp, pipe the dough directly into the hot oil without crowding the pan. Served with a cup of creamy Spanish hot chocolate, this simple indulgence leaves kids and adults alike with sugared fingertips, a big chocolate mustache, and a huge smile.

XURROS

½ cup whole milk

8 tablespoons (1 stick) unsalted butter, cut into 1-tablespoon pieces

1 cup all-purpose flour

5 large eggs

½ cup sugar

½ teaspoon ground aniseed

HOT CHOCOLATE

8 ounces dark chocolate (preferably 70% cacao), very finely chopped

4 teaspoons cornstarch

3 cups whole milk

2 teaspoons sugar

2 teaspoons pure vanilla extract

About 6 cups vegetable oil, for deep-frying

1   Prepare the xurros: In a medium saucepan, combine the milk, ½ cup of water, and the butter, and bring to a simmer over medium heat. Add the flour, stirring with a wooden spoon until a dough forms into a ball, leaving a thin coating of cooked flour on the bottom of the saucepan, 2 to 3 minutes. When you hear the dough begin to sizzle very softly, it has been cooked and stirred enough. Carefully transfer the hot dough to a stand mixer fitted with the paddle attachment. Mix on medium-low speed and, with the mixer running, add the eggs one at a time. Continue mixing until the dough is shiny, thick, and falls in golden ribbons from the paddle, 1 to 2 minutes.

2   Transfer the dough to a large pastry bag fitted with a large star tip (or a resealable bag with a corner snipped off). Combine the sugar and ground aniseed in a medium shallow bowl for coating the xurros.

3   Make the hot chocolate: In a small saucepan, toss together the chocolate and cornstarch. Place over medium-low heat and stir constantly until the chocolate begins to melt and soak up the cornstarch. Gently whisk in the milk and cook until the chocolate coats the back of a spoon, about 5 minutes. Stir in the sugar and vanilla until the sugar dissolves. Cover and set aside to keep warm.

4   Finish the xurros: Heat 2 inches of oil in a large Dutch oven over medium heat to 350°F. Adjust the heat as necessary to maintain the 350°F frying temperature. To form each xurro, pipe the dough into the hot oil in a loose swirl. Fry until puffed and golden brown on both sides, about 4 minutes, flipping once. As they are done, transfer the xurros to paper towels to drain briefly. While still warm, toss the xurros in the spiced sugar.

5   Pour the hot chocolate into small mugs and serve warm with the xurros on plates or a platter.

CARQUINYOLIS
CATALAN BISCOTTI

These classic cookies are very similar to Italian biscotti and such a staple in Catalan homes that they are even used in place of toasted bread in traditional *picades*. Try using two *carquinyolis* in place of the breadcrumbs in Rabbit and Mushroom Stew (page 166) or Meatballs with Cuttlefish (page 206) or in place of the almonds in Chicken with Shrimp (page 174). These cookies can be baked two ways: either in logs, then sliced and rebaked like Italian biscotti or, as written, baked only once. The single bake gives the carquinyolis an addictive, chewy texture and an appealing simplicity.

3 cups all-purpose flour, plus more for dusting

2 teaspoons baking soda

1⅓ cups sugar

½ cup (4 ounces) marzipan

1 teaspoon finely grated lemon zest

2 teaspoons ground cinnamon

½ cup whole milk or water

2 large eggs

2 cups Marcona almonds or regular skin-on almonds

1   Preheat the oven to 350°F. Line two sheet pans with parchment paper.

2   In a medium bowl, whisk together the flour and baking soda. In a stand mixer fitted with the paddle attachment, combine the sugar, marzipan, lemon zest, cinnamon, milk, and 1 of the eggs. Beat on medium speed until all the ingredients are combined. Stir in the flour mixture to combine, then stir in the almonds.

3   Lightly dust a clean work surface with flour. Turn out the dough and divide it into two equal portions. Pat each portion of dough into a 6-inch square about ½ inch thick, dusting your hands with flour as needed. Cut each square into 9 smaller squares (3 rows across by 3 rows down). Transfer the dough to the prepared sheet pans. In a small bowl, beat the remaining egg until smooth, then brush it over the top of each cookie.

4   Bake until the cookies are golden brown, shiny on top, and slightly puffed, about 30 minutes. Transfer to a wire rack to cool completely.

BUNYOLS DE QUARESMA
CATALAN DOUGHNUTS

The best part about making *bunyols* is that they don't have to be perfect. In fact, the word *bunyol* means "imperfect" in Catalan. These odd-shaped fritters are sold by the pound at bakeries around Lent. As a kid, I couldn't get enough of them and was always excited to find one still warm. Anise is the signature flavor—around Barcelona, they use ground aniseed. I like to use ground star anise for a similar yet different flavor. Serve the fritters with chocolate sauce for dunking, if you like, or stuff them with pastry cream.

4 star anise

2 cups all-purpose flour, plus more for your hands

½ teaspoon ground cinnamon

1 teaspoon finely grated lemon zest

5 large egg yolks

1 cup sugar

1 envelope (¼ ounce) active dry yeast

1 teaspoon kosher salt

½ cup lukewarm whole milk

4 tablespoons lard or unsalted butter, at room temperature

About 6 cups vegetable oil, for deep-frying, plus more for the dough

¼ cup anisette or other anise liqueur

1   Place the star anise in a mortar or spice grinder and pound or pulse until finely ground. Measure out ½ teaspoon of the ground star anise (set the remainder aside). In a medium bowl, whisk together the ½ teaspoon star anise, the flour, cinnamon, and lemon zest.

2   In the bowl of a stand mixer, whisk together (by hand) the egg yolks, ½ cup of the sugar, and the yeast. Add the flour mixture. Snap on the dough hook and mix on medium speed until the ingredients are combined. With the mixer running, sprinkle in the salt, then pour in the milk. Mix and knead until the dough is springy, tight, and firm, like a baby's cheek, 5 minutes. Add the lard and mix just until blended into the dough. Use a bench scraper or silicone spatula to pull the dough away from sides of the bowl and form it into a compact ball.

(recipe continues)

3   Drizzle a large bowl with a bit of vegetable oil and add the dough. Drizzle a little more oil over the dough, turning the ball to coat it with a thin film of oil. Cover the bowl with a damp towel and set it aside in a warm spot to rise to double its size, about 2 hours.

4   Pour a bit of oil onto a work surface to coat. Turn out the dough and roll it into a log 3 inches in diameter. Cut the log crosswise into 12 to 15 pieces and roll each piece into a ball. Place the balls on an oiled sheet pan, spacing them about 2 inches apart. Let the dough sit, uncovered, in a warm spot until doubled in size, 1 to 2 hours.

5   Oil the work surface again. Bring the pan of risen dough portions to your work area and place one ball on it. Dip a finger in flour and poke a hole into the center of the dough, pressing all the way through to the work surface. Spin your finger in circles, gently twirling the dough like a hula hoop, to create a rustic doughnut hole. Repeat with the remaining dough.

6   Heat 2 inches of vegetable oil in a large Dutch oven over medium heat to 350°F. Adjust the heat as necessary to maintain the 350°F frying temperature. Working in batches, add the doughnuts and fry until puffed and golden brown on both sides, 2 to 3 minutes per batch, turning with tongs or a slotted spoon. Remove the doughnuts to paper towels to drain as they are done.

7   In a medium bowl, stir together the remaining ½ cup sugar and the remaining ground star anise. While the doughnuts are still warm, drizzle them all over with the liqueur, then immediately transfer them to the sugar mixture. Toss them in the spiced sugar to coat. Serve warm or at room temperature.

CREMA CATALANA
CATALAN CUSTARDS

SERVES 6

Crema Catalana is just lemon custard, but to me it's more than that. It is a symbol of happiness in Catalonia. This dessert is like a cross between pots de crème and crème brûlée, with subtle aromas of cinnamon and lemon. The caramelized top is traditionally formed by holding a glowing hot iron over the sugar, but a kitchen torch also works. Start these custards at least the morning before you plan to serve them—or up to 3 days ahead—as they need time to chill before serving.

2 cinnamon sticks

1 quart heavy cream

Zest of 3 medium lemons, peeled off in large strips with a vegetable peeler

Pinch of kosher salt

¾ cup plus 6 tablespoons sugar

8 large egg yolks, at room temperature

1   Place the cinnamon sticks in a medium saucepan and toast over medium heat until they smell intensely sweet and turn slightly darker, about 2 minutes, shaking the pan and rolling the sticks occasionally for even browning. Remove the pan from the heat. Add the cream, lemon zest, salt, and ¾ cup of the sugar. Return to medium-high heat and bring to a boil, then remove the saucepan from the heat and let the mixture steep for at least 1 hour at room temperature or as long as overnight in the refrigerator for more flavor. Remove the cinnamon sticks and lemon zest.

2   Preheat the oven to 275°F.

3   Reheat the cream in the saucepan over low heat until warmed through, 3 to 4 minutes. In a medium bowl, beat the egg yolks until smooth. Whisking constantly, pour the warm cream into the egg yolks in a very thin stream until combined.

4   Arrange six 6-ounce ramekins in a 13 × 9-inch baking dish. Fill the ramekins three-quarters of the way with the custard mixture. Transfer the baking dish to a pulled-out oven rack and pour enough hot water into the baking dish to come about halfway up the sides of the ramekins. Close the oven and bake until the custards are firm yet jiggly in the middle when tested with a quick shake, 45 to 50 minutes. Remove the ramekins from the water bath and let cool completely, about 1 hour. Cover the cooled ramekins with plastic wrap, without the plastic touching the custard, and refrigerate until cold, at least 2 hours or up to 3 days.

5 Just before serving, sprinkle a thin layer of sugar (about 1 tablespoon) over the custard in each ramekin. Use a kitchen torch to melt and caramelize the sugar, moving the flame constantly over the surface. If you don't have a kitchen torch, you can caramelize the sugar by placing the ramekins on a sheet pan and placing the sheet pan 4 to 6 inches beneath a hot broiler for a few minutes. The sugar will go from white to amber caramel, and when it cools, the caramel will form a thin, crackling crust. Serve immediately.

ARRÒS AMB LLET
CATALAN RICE PUDDING

My grandmother would often make this dish for me and leave leftovers in the refrigerator. I would sneak a taste as often as I could. After coming in from a day in the hot summer sun, it made the most refreshing snack. It's amazing how familiar ingredients—just sugar, cinnamon, rice, and milk—can blend together to make something so comforting.

1 cup Spanish rice, such as bomba
¼ teaspoon kosher salt
1 quart half-and-half
¼ cup packed light brown sugar
¼ cup granulated sugar
1 vanilla bean, split lengthwise
2 cinnamon sticks
1 lemon

1   In a small saucepan, combine the rice, salt, and 2 cups of water. Cover and bring to a boil over high heat, 3 to 4 minutes, stirring a few times to prevent sticking. As soon as the water comes to a boil, remove from the heat and drain the rice in a medium-mesh strainer.

2   Meanwhile, in a medium saucepan, combine the half-and-half, brown sugar, and granulated sugar. Scrape the vanilla seeds into the pan and add the vanilla pod along with 1 of the cinnamon sticks. Use a vegetable peeler to pull the zest from half of the lemon in long wide strips, taking care to remove only the yellow part and not the bitter white pith underneath. Add the lemon strips to the pan and place the pan over medium heat. Cook until the sugar dissolves, 2 to 3 minutes, stirring occasionally. Stir in the rice, cover, and bring the mixture to a boil over medium-high heat, stirring once or twice. Uncover, reduce the heat to medium-low, and simmer gently until the rice is tender, 20 to 25 minutes, stirring frequently to prevent sticking on the bottom of the pan.

3   Use tongs to remove and discard the vanilla pod, cinnamon stick, and lemon strips. Pour the hot rice mixture into four to six ramekins or custard cups and press plastic wrap directly onto the rice pudding, wrapping each serving tightly. Refrigerate until well chilled. Serve cold or at room temperature with some freshly grated lemon zest from the remaining lemon half and freshly grated cinnamon from the remaining cinnamon stick.

GELAT DE XOCOLATA

DARK CHOCOLATE ICE CREAM WITH
CHOCOLATE-COVERED MARCONA ALMONDS

MAKES 1 QUART
ICE CREAM

When we visit Catalonia in the summer, my kids chase after ice cream treats similar to this one. The chocolate-covered Marcona almonds elevate it a notch above your typical chocolate ice cream. Make this dessert a day ahead so it has time to freeze properly and achieve a creamy texture. I like to eat the ice cream drizzled with olive oil, some flaky sea salt, and a pinch of freshly ground black pepper.

1½ cups whole milk

1½ cups heavy cream

1½ teaspoons pure vanilla paste (see note)

¾ cup sugar

¾ teaspoon kosher salt

½ cup unsweetened cocoa powder

8 ounces dark chocolate (around 75% cacao), finely chopped

4 large egg yolks, at room temperature

1 cup salted Marcona almonds

1 In a medium saucepan, stir together the milk, cream, vanilla paste, sugar, salt, and cocoa powder. Bring to a simmer over medium heat, then remove the pan from the heat and stir in 4 ounces of the chocolate. Cover the pan and set aside until the chocolate melts, about 5 minutes. Stir until the melted chocolate is fully incorporated into the cream mixture. Set aside.

2 Set a medium bowl into a larger bowl of ice and water. In a separate medium bowl, whisk the egg yolks with ½ cup of the warm chocolate mixture. Scrape the mixture back into the saucepan, whisking to combine. Return the pan to medium-low heat and cook gently until the custard coats the back of a spoon, 10 to 12 minutes, stirring almost constantly.

3 Strain the hot custard through a fine-mesh strainer into the bowl in the ice bath. Stir the custard occasionally to help cool it down. When the custard is cooled, after about 5 minutes, press plastic onto the surface and refrigerate the custard until it is cold, at least 4 hours or overnight.

(recipe continues)

4   To make the chocolate-covered almonds, line a large sheet pan with parchment or a nonstick silicone baking mat. Place the remaining 4 ounces chocolate in a heatproof bowl that is large enough to sit over (but not in) a medium saucepan of water to create a double boiler. Bring the water to a boil over high heat (without the bowl of chocolate on top), then reduce the heat to medium-low to simmer steadily. Place the bowl of chocolate over the simmering water and stir just until melted, about 8 minutes. Stir the almonds into the melted chocolate until thoroughly coated. Pour the coated almonds out onto the prepared sheet pan, spreading them in a single layer. Set aside to cool to room temperature, about 20 minutes. Transfer the sheet pan to the refrigerator and chill until the chocolate sets, about 20 minutes more. Transfer the chocolate-covered almonds to a cutting board and roughly chop.

5   Pour the chilled custard mixture into an ice cream maker and churn according to the manufacturer's instructions. When the mixture reaches the consistency of a thick milkshake, mix in the chopped almonds. Working quickly, scrape the churned ice cream mixture into an airtight container and transfer to the freezer to set. This ice cream tastes best when served within 5 days, if you can resist it for that long.

EL CONSELL: To avoid adding water to the ice cream, I prefer to use vanilla paste, which is essentially a jar of vanilla bean scrapings suspended in thick syrup. Look for vanilla paste in well-stocked supermarkets or online. You can use about 2 teaspoons vanilla extract instead, but the ice cream may develop a slightly icier texture as a result.

MEL I MATÓ

HONEY AND MATÓ CHEESECAKE

Mel i Mató is a simple, ancient Catalan dessert of honey drizzled over soft cheese. Mató is strained, often house-made cheese usually made from goat's milk and cow's milk. It is similar to crumbly ricotta and is typically sliced, scattered with walnuts, and drizzled with honey. Mel i Mató reminds me of the Montserrat mountain (see pages 248–49) because there local Catalans sell it to eager tourists along with unusual treats like herbal aperitif drinks. The mountainside version is pretty rustic, but I use the same flavors to turn this classic combination into something more festive: a goat cheese cheesecake layered over walnut torte.

WALNUT TORTE

8 tablespoons (1 stick) unsalted butter, melted and cooled, plus more for the pan

½ cup walnut halves

¼ cup all-purpose flour

¼ cup semolina flour

½ teaspoon baking powder

½ teaspoon kosher salt

½ teaspoon finely grated orange zest

2 large eggs

½ cup sugar

¼ cup fresh orange juice

CHEESECAKE TOPPING

1 tablespoon unflavored powdered gelatin

1 cup whole milk

¾ cup sugar

1 teaspoon kosher salt

1 cup (8 ounces) fresh goat cheese, at room temperature, cut into 4 large pieces

2 large egg yolks, at room temperature

2 cups heavy cream

About ¾ cup honey, for serving

1   Make the torte: Preheat the oven to 350°F. Grease a 9-inch springform pan with butter. Line the bottom and sides of the pan with parchment (cut a round of parchment for the bottom of the pan and cut a wide strip of parchment to line the sides).

2   In a food processor, combine the walnuts, both flours, the baking powder, salt, and orange zest. Pulse until the walnuts are finely ground.

3   In a stand mixer fitted with the paddle attachment, beat the whole eggs and sugar on medium speed until light in texture, pale yellow in color, and the mixture falls from the paddle in thick ribbons, about 3 minutes. With the speed on low, add the melted butter in a thin stream, mixing until combined. Still with the mixer running on low, add half the flour mixture, followed by the orange juice, followed by the remaining flour mixture.

(recipe continues)

4 Pour the batter into the prepared pan and set on a sheet pan. Bake until the torte is golden around the edges, 30 to 35 minutes. Set aside to cool completely on a wire rack, about 1 hour.

5 Meanwhile, make the cheesecake topping: Place ¼ cup of water in a medium bowl. Sprinkle the gelatin over the top and let it stand, without stirring, until the gelatin absorbs the water and swells into a stiff gel, about 5 minutes.

6 In a medium saucepan, bring the milk, sugar, and salt to a simmer over medium heat. Cook, stirring, until the sugar dissolves.

7 Place the goat cheese and egg yolks in a blender or food processor. Add about ½ cup of the warm milk mixture and blend until smooth. Return the mixture to the saucepan and cook until the custard coats the back of a spoon, about 3 minutes, stirring constantly. Strain the hot custard through a fine-mesh strainer into the bowl with the gelatin. Whisk until the gelatin and custard are smooth. Set aside to cool until the custard is just warm to the touch, about 20 minutes—it will thicken significantly as it cools.

8 While the custard cools, place the cream in the bowl of a stand mixer fitted with the whisk attachment and beat until soft peaks form, about 2 minutes.

9 Whisk about half of the whipped cream into the cooled custard until combined. Use a rubber spatula to gently fold in the remaining whipped cream. Pour the cheesecake topping over the cooled torte in the pan and transfer to the refrigerator until firm and set, about 1 hour.

10 Unhinge the springform and remove the parchment lining from the sides of the cake. Dip a long, sharp knife in hot water to slice the cake. Transfer the slices to plates and drizzle each serving with about 1 tablespoon honey.

FLAM DE TORRÓ
MINIATURE TURRÓN FLANS

Around the holidays, every Catalan bakery sells torró, a traditional Christmas dessert of almond and honey nougat. If I forget to bring some back with me when I'm visiting, I look for it online (which you can do, too). I like to incorporate torró into these flans by pureeing it with hot syrup until it's thick and creamy. The texture and almond flavor give these flans a unique twist.

¾ cup sugar

Kosher salt

⅓ cup whole milk

1½ ounces torró, finely chopped (⅓ cup)

7 large egg yolks, at room temperature

1 Preheat the oven to 275°F.

2 In a small skillet, combine ¼ cup of the sugar, 2 tablespoons water, and a pinch of salt and cook over medium-low heat, stirring, until the sugar dissolves. Increase the heat and bring to a boil. Cook until the syrup turns light amber, about 5 minutes, swirling the pan occasionally for even browning. Carefully swirl in the milk (it will bubble wildly).

3 Divide the hot caramel among 12 tall, narrow, ¼-cup custard cups or ramekins, using about 1½ teaspoons in each. Set aside.

4 In a small saucepan, bring the remaining ½ cup sugar and ½ cup water to a boil over high heat until the sugar dissolves. Place the torró in a blender or food processor and pour the hot sugar syrup in. Blend until the nougat breaks down, the mixture develops a golden color, and the consistency is that of heavy cream. Add the egg yolks and blend again until smooth (the custard will separate slightly with a bit of white foam on top).

5 Place the ramekins in a large rectangular baking dish and pour the custard into each ramekin on top of the caramel. Transfer the baking dish to a pulled-out oven rack and pour enough hot water into the baking dish to come about halfway up the sides of the ramekins. Close the oven and bake until the custards are firm throughout and a knife inserted in the center of one comes out clean, about 35 minutes. Remove the custards from the water bath and let cool for 10 minutes. Run a sharp knife along the inside of the ramekins to loosen the custards. Invert each ramekin onto a plate or tray to unmold. Cover the cooled custards with plastic wrap, then refrigerate until well chilled, at least 2 hours or up to 3 days. You can also unmold and freeze them.

ACKNOWLEDGMENTS

FROM D.O.–

To all the farmers, fishermen, bread makers, butchers, shepherds, and everyone involved in the *creation* of food in Catalunya; without their hands we could not survive. Nature dictates the seasons, but following the seasons and learning their flavors is a passion that all these people bring to us.

To my family, and especially my wife, Vanessa, for always supporting my career and being the best mother a family could ever dream of. To my sister, Gloria, for her help and understanding, and for taking care of our parents while I was writing this book.

To my mom, Encarna, who gave me the tools to be good with my senses and taste everything fully. She went out of her way to cook for us and to feed us well while we were very humble.

To my dad, Ton, for working so hard to pay for all my eating habits as a kid and for showing me what it meant to be a true Catalan. He was not able to see this book finished, but hopefully the words and recipes here honor his birthplace, Penedès, the egg yolk of the world.

To all the people who have helped me shape my style and become who I am professionally: first, my uncle Paco Sánchez, who taught me a lot about discipline and organization; my chef colleagues, friends, and professionals—Fermí Puig, Judy Rodgers, Ritsu Tsuchida, Quim Marquès, Jordi Vila, Adrià Marín, Josep Cudié, Miquel Mata, Bernat Franco, Núria Ruiz, Marc Parés, Gaby Parés, Salvador Valls, Salvador "Lero" Queraltó, Raimon "Totxo" Palau, Carles Diego; and my Barlata team. A big thank-you to my great friend Jaume Rafecas, a professor of Catalan language, for jumping up to help correct the Catalan spellings every time I showed up in Vilafranca with the manuscript.

Special thanks to the Ajuntament de Vilafranca, to Pere, who was always there for me, to the Castellers de Vilafranca for always embracing me, Restaurant Platets (we ate there *a lot*), Cal Ton, L'Ateneu (love their *popurri*), Pepe Raventós, Gessi Llopart, Joan Cusiné, Marcel Sabaté, Santi Bundó, Joan Pona, and Jesús Trotonda.

To all the mothers of my friends from Vilafranca and all the little towns surrounding it who fed me as a kid, thanks for inviting me to dinner.

To Michelle Rodarte for instigating this book, Lisa Ekus for believing in the project, and Amanda Englander, Stephanie Huntwork, and the rest of the amazing team at Clarkson Potter for taking this book to the next level. To Caroline Wright and Johnny Autry; without their love for Catalonia, their smiles, hugs, and big belly laughs, this book could not have been possible. And last, thank you to David Joachim for joining us near the end of the writing to help us finish this project. I can't imagine finding a better person to carry our dream through to the end.

During the creation of the book, my father passed away, my mother had a stroke, and I had a major bicycle accident. Also, my writing partner, Caroline, was diagnosed with brain cancer and my agent, Lisa, was diagnosed with breast cancer. To them go my heartfelt thoughts of peace. Despite the challenges we faced, life went on, and I am inspired by them and honored that their beautiful spirits continue to shine here in this book.

FROM C.W.–

Writing this book, for me, had two chapters. One came from imagining and creating this dream project and the dream team that worked on it. The other came from a team who supported this book (and me) when I was diagnosed with brain cancer just before the manuscript was finished.

Michelle, my first *salud* belongs to you for introducing me to Daniel and for being the first person to believe in this project, as well as the superhero who pushed the project forward when I had to step back.

To a woman who has already given so much to my career, Anne Willan: Thank you for lending enthusiasm and guidance to this project in its earliest stages and for your continued support.

To Lisa (and Sally and our friends at TLEG) for picking up where Anne left off and helping me find the right words and team to honor Daniel's story, and then for helping me find even more teammates when I needed to hand over this project. You really are saviors, each of you.

To Amanda, thank you for being a champion of this project from the very beginning and, later, of me, when I learned of my diagnosis. Knowing that you were at the helm and had a vision for the finished book, I could rest and let the project pass from my hands to other collaborators. You helped give me peace and space as I began to fight my cancer, and for that I am deeply grateful.

This brings me to my most heartfelt thanks, to David Joachim, the kind writer who stepped in to clean up our Catalan party and make our work brighter and stronger while I was recovering from surgery and facing rounds of chemotherapy. Without him, this book might never have been finished. Without him, the collective dream held in these pages could have been lost. That he was involved felt like a miracle, both personally to me and for the quality of the finished book. I am sincerely grateful such a thoughtful and talented writer was able to step in and join our crazy team.

La meva familia: So much of my thanks and adoration goes to Daniel, of course, for letting me into his world and stay for a nibble or two. You are a treasure whose *collons* are as big as your heart. I have joined the mass of people who are so proud to know you and who would stop you in the street to tell you so. I can't believe the journey this book took us on. What a beautiful dream it has been and continues to be in these pages. I just wish it involved fewer hospitals.

Johnny, *el Guapo*, I was lucky to have you as a running partner in our race across Catalonia. I hope you are reading this alongside an American-size coffee. Your pictures are the beauty I will always hold in my heart for Catalonia. You are as kind as you are talented, my friend, and I am truly honored to have worked together. *Vinga!*

To the silent helpers, our families, who allowed us to carve out time from our very busy schedules to make this book: first, to my dad and mom, Paul and Glad Markunas, for taking care of my life when I couldn't, and for being superstar grandparents as I wrote these pages. For that, I owe you another Thanksgiving in Santa Fe and the year of sanity that I borrowed from you to be able to write this book as a tumor was growing in my brain. To my boys, Garth, Henry, and Theodore, for being gracious and kind and encouraging, always, and willing to eat Catalan food any night of the week for the years I worked on this book. Each of you is a lens through which I see beauty and my desire to create it, now and always, and I hope this book is a reminder of that truth. To my Seattle tribe who took shifts with my boys in the eleventh hour when I first wrote these pages and who continue to hold me up in the kindest, brightest light: Al, Katy, Katie, Ellen, and Adair. To Vanessa and Charlotte for making it possible for Daniel and Johnny to focus on our project as we traveled and spent so much time and money chasing this thing we had to make, and for your support when plans changed yet again.

To Kate Wilson, for your sisterhood and diligent recipe testing. A big thanks, too, to the team at Barlata who let me ask a million persistent questions as they made paella and *braves*.

Daniel tells me miracles can happen with a lot of saliva and patience. This book was that miracle for me—the start of a really beautiful, really wild ride I never could have imagined myself. I am grateful and honored to have been a part of it all and so thankful for everyone who helped me along the way.

RESOURCES

AMAZON
amazon.com
Its collection of third-party vendors makes it a helpful resource.

CATALAN GOURMET
1133 Broadway, Suite 1614
New York, NY 10010
646-719-0061
catalangourmet.com
Ham, sausage, fish, cheese, olive oil, vinegar, spices, and more.

DESPAÑA BRAND IMPORTS
60-01 31st Avenue
Woodside, NY 11377
718-779-4971
despanabrandfoods.com/shop
Nice selection of *vermut* accompaniments, including *latas*, *conserves*, *picos*, Marcona almonds, *ñora* chiles, and cured meats.

LA ESPAÑOLA MEATS, INC.
25020 Doble Avenue
Harbor City, CA 90710
310-539-0455
laespanolameats.tienda/en
Spanish chorizo, rice, pimentón, and more.

LA TIENDA
3601 La Grange Parkway
Toano, VA 23168
800-710-4304
tienda.com
Full array of imported Spanish foods, including good-quality sofregit and fresh Ibérico specialty cuts, such as *secreto* and tenderloin.

MARKET HALL FOODS
5655 College Avenue, Suite 201
Oakland, CA 94618
888-952-4005
markethallfoods.com
Specialty extra-virgin olive oils and vinegars, such as PX.

THE SPANISH TABLE
1814 San Pablo Avenue
Berkeley, CA 94702
510-548-1383
spanishtable.com
Wide variety of Spanish cookware, food, and wines such as cava, vermouth, and sherry.

YAYA IMPORTS
530 Boulder Court #105
Pleasanton, CA 94566
925-249-9292
yayaimports.com
Paella pans, rice, and other Spanish imports.

EQUIVALENTS AND CONVERSIONS

OVEN TEMPERATURES

CELCIUS	GAS MARK (UK)	FAHRENHEIT
120	½	250
140	1	275
150	2	300
160	3	325
180	4	350
190	5	375
200	6	400
220	7	425
230	8	450
240	9	475
260	10	500

LIQUID (VOLUME) CONVERSIONS

METRIC	UK IMPERIAL	US
30 milliliters	1 fluid ounce	2 tablespoons
60 milliliters	2 fluid ounces	¼ cup
75 milliliters	2½ fluid ounces	⅓ cup
125 milliliters	4 fluid ounces	½ cup
150 milliliters	5 fluid ounces	⅔ cup
175 milliliters	6 fluid ounces	¾ cup
250 milliliters	8 fluid ounces	1 cup
300 milliliters	10 fluid ounces (½ pint)	1¼ cups
375 milliliters	12 fluid ounces	1½ cups
400 milliliters	13 fluid ounces	1⅔ cups
425 milliliters	14 fluid ounces	1¾ cups
500 milliliters	16 fluid ounces	2 cups
625 milliliters	20 fluid ounces (1 pint)	2½ cups
750 milliliters	1¼ pints	3 cups
1 liter	35 fluid ounces (1¾ pints)	4 cups (1 quart)
1.25 liters	40 fluid ounces (1 quart)	5 cups
1.5 liters	50 fluid ounces (1¼ quarts)	6 cups
2 liters	70 fluid ounces (1¾ quarts)	8 cups (2 quarts)

INDEX

Note: Page references in *italics* indicate photographs.

DANIEL OLIVELLA is a chef born in Vilafranca del Penedès near Barcelona and has nearly 40 years of experience cooking authentic Catalan food for the American palate. Considered an authority on Mediterranean cuisine by many, Olivella worked for some of the best chefs in San Francisco, where he opened the popular Catalan bistro B44 in 1999. He is currently the chef and owner of Barlata in Austin, Texas, where he lives with his family.

Also available as an ebook

COVER DESIGN: STEPHANIE HUNTWORK
COVER PHOTOGRAPHS: JOHNNY AUTRY

CLARKSON POTTER/PUBLISHERS
New York
clarksonpotter.com